THE FILMS OF

JOHN WAYNE

LUMETTA

THE FILMS OF
JOHN WAYNE

by
Mark Ricci,
Boris Zmijewsky,
and
Steve Zmijewsky

THE CITADEL PRESS
Secaucus, New Jersey

PHOTO ACKNOWLEDGMENTS

Carlos Clarens, Dion McGregor, Irving Wolfe, Richard Husking, Jr. Miss Ushak of the Museum of Modern Art, MGM-Loew's, Inc., 20th Century-Fox, Paramount, Universal, Warner Bros., Columbia, RKO, Republic, Monogram, United Artists, and Marc Cutler.

Ninth paperbound printing, 1979

Published by Citadel Press
A division of Lyle Stuart, Inc.
In Canada: George J. McLeod Limited
73 Bathurst St., Toronto, Ont.
Manufactured in the United States of America
Designed by C. R. Bloodgood
ISBN 0-8065-0296-7

Dedicated to
JOHN FORD
the prophet

Contents

✓ wheel of Fortune (1940s?)

Introduction

Introduction

"When the legend becomes a fact, print the legend!"
—*The Man Who Shot Liberty Valance*

John Wayne, who bore the name of Marion Michael Morrison for the first twenty-some years of his life, was born May 26, 1908 in Winterset, Iowa. When he was five years old, his father, Clyde Morrison, lost his health and the family doctor recommended a sojourn in the desert. So when the elder Morrison, a pharmacist, gathered up his wife Mary and his young son and his belongings and moved to Lancaster, California, a town near the barren Mojave Desert, young John got his first taste of ranch life.

One year of homesteading gave the elder Morrison back his health, so he moved his family to Glendale and opened up a drugstore. John and his younger brother Bob grew up in the famous Los Angeles suburb. By now young John already earned the nickname Duke because, as the story goes, young John would always be seen with a big dog called Duke and folks, seeing them together all the time, got to calling him Little Duke.

Wayne was an outstanding student all through his school years. At Glendale High he acted in some of the school plays and he was also one of the stars of the football team. His goal in his senior year was to get an appointment to the Naval Academy at

Annapolis. He came close, but missed out. A naval career had been his boyhood ambition and to forget his disappointment he stowed away on an ocean liner bound for Honolulu. Following this brief escapade he worked as an apricot picker, truck driver and ice man.

Then he was able to secure a college scholarship at the University of Southern California. He became a star Trojan tackle in the era of the great USC football teams.

John worked in the prop department at Fox Studios during summer vacations. However, it was the famous Western star Tom Mix who got John into the movie business and not Director John Ford as popularly supposed, though Ford is the man responsible for making Wayne into a screen star and the top box-office personality of the industry and Wayne reveres the brilliant director as his personal prophet.

"Tom Mix gave me my first movie job," Wayne said. "I was attending the University of Southern California, playing tackle on the football team. My father, who lived in Glendale, was having a tough time. The depression had started and he simply was not a good businessman, although a fine man and a wonderful father. He had opened a new drugstore in Glendale, and it failed. An ice cream company also failed.

"Howard Jones, the Trojan football coach, heard that I needed a job. It seems that Jones had arranged for Mix, a football enthusiast, to get some choice seats, and the grateful actor had promised the coach he'd get some of his players jobs that summer.

"I was given a job with the 'swing gang,' a sort of utility work outfit. My wages were $35 a week. My job was to lug furniture and props around to arrange them on the set.

"The first picture I worked on I remember was *Mother Machree* which John Ford was directing."

Wayne was sweeping up fake snow after a heartbreaking winter scene in *Mother Machree*. Thinking a scene was finished, Wayne walked onto the set and started to make the corn flakes fly with his trusty broom. He was interrupted by the loud and angry shouts of the director, John Ford, who pointed to the camera and berated him as seven kinds of idiot. The look on Wayne's face soon had Ford laughing, and the noted director invited him to lunch that afternoon. That was the beginning of Wayne's movie acting career.

Wayne continued working in the prop department and now and then as a stuntman. He also began to get bit parts in Ham Hamilton comedies and Ford films such as *Hangman's House, Salute, Men Without Women.* His hero-worship of John Ford was born around this time and continues to this day.

During the filming of *Men Without Women,* being made at sea off the California coast near Catalina Island, Ford was running into a little difficulty. The script called for professional stuntmen to perform feats of heroism in the rough, high waters, which grow rougher by the hour. Noticing the stuntmen balking, Ford called his fourth assistant propertyman, busy at work on the second deck.

"Show 'em up," he yelled.

Without hesitation, pliers and hammer still in hand, Wayne made the jump into the waves. John Wayne was never to disobey a direction from John Ford.

Raoul Walsh was looking for a tall, gangling newcomer with a peculiar loping stride to star in his next picture, *The Big Trail.* John Ford induced Walsh to come over and look at his prop man and part-time actor. Ford pointed to Wayne and said, "There's your man!"

Raoul Walsh signed Wayne to star in the first feature to use a new film process, called Grandeur Screen, which was 70mm film. Fox Studios changed his name from Marion Morrison to John Wayne because the studio heads couldn't see a guy named Marion as the fastest gun in the West. And, besides, John Wayne had a nice honest sound to it. The first brick in the foundation of the career of John Wayne was laid—the nom-de-film "John Wayne" was born.

Soon after he signed for the part, Wayne made his first important mistake. Lacking acting experience, but eager to please, he hunted up a drama coach and took some intensive training. Then he reported to work with a full equipment of exaggerated gestures and fancy dramatic stances.

Walsh spent the next two weeks working the ham

out of Wayne. He finally convinced Wayne that he didn't want acting. He justed wanted him to act naturally.

His first scene ever in a Western was a literal eye-opener for the ex-college football star who made a fetish of always being in condition. He was supposed to be riding alongside a wagon train as Tully Marshall, a character actor, comes up to him and offers him a drink.

But Marshall took his role seriously and as Wayne approached, he could see that Tully was drunk. Marshall, however, didn't falter. He handed Wayne his jug, as he was supposed to, and Wayne took a deep swallow. Instead of water or tea, that jug was full of the worst rot-gut. There was nothing Wayne could do but swallow it all down or ruin the whole scene.

The Big Trail was not a financial success. Through an error in judgment, the wide-screen process sank the picture before it had a chance. At that time it was felt that large screens would replace the smaller variety throughout the country. But this didn't happen. The theatre-owners were already digging deep into their pockets to pay for sound equipment, and the depression was beginning. Shown only in a few large cities in 70mm, it was later released in 35mm version but still didn't recoup the money invested in it.

Though the picture failed to make money, it was a "big picture" and thus an auspicious start in featured roles for John Wayne. His employers were sufficiently impressed to give him a second role. He was casted in a pot-boiler festively called *Girls Demand Excitement*. The high point of its unepic plot was a basketball game between the boys' and girls' teams. Wayne read the script and shuddered. He was later to call this picture the worst ever made. Then, while brooding over his less-than-happy lot, he was accosted by a Fox co-worker, Will Rogers.

"What's your problem?" Will politely inquired. Wayne explained that his part was not a good one.

"What?" said Will with a grin and shrug. "You workin', ain't you?"

In 1931, after two pictures for Fox, Wayne departed Fox Film Studios for Columbia Pictures, starting with such Western heroes as Buck Jones and Tim McCoy. Not until Wayne is a Super Star in the 1950's does he return to Fox, appearing in John Huston's *The Barbarian and the Geisha*.

In 1932 Wayne went to Warner Brothers to do a series of "B" Westerns in which he was the star. For nearly ten years Wayne ground out a succession of low-budget Westerns.

"Each one" says Wayne, "was lousier than the last."

Slowly, Wayne drifted down the scale of Hollywood caste. When he got an offer from Mascot Films to do serials he ruefully accepted. Now he was slaving in the salt-mines of Hollywood—"Poverty Row"—where they worked on low budgets, fast schedules and pretty low-grade films.

Mascot Pictures Corporation, later to become the nucleus of the Republic Organization, turned out three serials with Wayne: *Shadow of the Eagle, Hurricane Express* and *The Three Musketeers.* Each one was fast-moving and tightly budgeted and completed in twenty-one days each.

During this period Wayne married Josephine Saenz. They set up housekeeping in a small furnished apartment. She was the daughter of a Panamanian diplomat. It was a rather "social" marriage for the "three and one-half day" Western star, but otherwise obscure young man.

About the time Wayne was getting bored with being tied to railroad tracks and finding himself in strange rooms where the walls contracted and squeezed you to death at the end of the chapter, Trem Carr, production head at Monogram, decided Wayne had a good face for Westerns. So they took Wayne out of the cobra pits, mounted him on a horse, gave him a trusty six-shooter and he became a Western star. And it was almost that easy.

Wayne made at least eight pictures a year for the next ten years. The first picture under the banner of Lone Star/Monogram cost a total of $11,000—including everything. The budget was so tight they couldn't afford more than one horse. So in the first scene Wayne knocks out the heavy and steals his horse (which he stole from the heroine's brother in the first place).

"I've been in more bad pictures than just about anyone in the business," said John Wayne. "But it doesn't matter. As long as you project yourself, and you're not mean or petty, the public will forgive you."

These early Westerns, all fast-paced rugged little action dramas, were valuable training for Wayne. Through countless canyons, valleys, plains, and trails

big and small, he rode and fought, learning his craft and growing slowly but steadily into star category. A long and rugged apprenticeship for the once and future king of all Westerns.

Limited mostly to action-fans, these Westerns were seen and quickly forgotten at the local theatres. Wayne had little opportunity to be exposed to a wider movie audience, but his star was rising. In 1935, Republic Pictures was born, and as the studio moved to establish itself as the foremost independent studio of its time, the firm did its share to develop new, profitable screen players and promote the current ones like John Wayne. Republic upgraded each successive Wayne picture and at the same time loaned him out to other film studios.

Meanwhile, Wayne met Yakima Canutt, a rodeo rider and movie stuntman. Canutt taught Wayne all his tricks, including how to fall from a running horse without being hurt. Together they sweated out the technique of barroom brawling. They studied the right way to draw and shoot a gun.

"I even copied Yak's smooth-rolling walk," said Wayne. "And the way he talks kinda low and with quiet strength."

Credit for the pace and pulse-jolting realism of Wayne's screen fights goes to Canutt. When they're ready to shoot, Canutt comes in and takes over. He works out the action, lines up the camera and directs the scene.

"Yak," says Wayne, "is the best fighter, horse rider and stuntman who ever lived. I've been learnin' from him for years."

Wayne and Canutt developed and perfected the screen-fight technique now generally in use. They discovered that near-miss swings, with the fist smacks dubbed on the soundtrack, could be made to look real when photographed at an angle. The bone-crunching illusion of today's cinema barroom brawls, as compared with the pale fakes of early movies, is not the least of Wayne's contributions to the art. He also is credited with having broken the taboo against a Western hero's use of anything but his fists in combat. Now heroes smash chairs and tables over villain's heads with wild abandon.

In 1936 Republic started the best series of Westerns ever produced, *The Three Mesquiteers.* They were very profitable, both to the studio and the theatres that showed them. Between riding herd for

Republic, John was loaned out to Universal Pictures for five films, all non-Westerns (*Conflict, California Straight Ahead, I Cover the War, Idol of the Crowds* and *Adventure's End*), and in 1938 continued the Mesquiteer series.

A star in his own films since 1932, Wayne was approaching his tenth year in films, and still he was riding the wide range of "B" movies, with the uplift to "A" movies nowhere in sight.

A thought must have crossed Wayne's mind that he may remain in the land of the "B" Western forever, like the countless other Western heroes riding the celluloid plains: Charles Starrett, Tex Ritter, Bob Steele, Gene Autry, Roy Rogers.

But Fate and John Ford had other plans for John Wayne, "the idol of young America" (as an early 'thirties pressbook proclaimed in the press releases).

The subject of John Ford is a touchy one with Wayne, and he feels guilty if he says anything "unloyal," somewhat like a grown son reminiscing about a tyrannical but beloved father.

"I worked on and off for years in menial jobs for him," said Wayne, "as a prop boy, stuntman, bit player. I developed a hero worship that still exists. But when I got stuck in three and one-half day Westerns, Ford passed me by without speaking. This went on for three years, he just wouldn't look at me. Then, one day, I was at a waterfront bar when Ford's daughter appeared and said, "Father wants you on his yacht." I didn't know what to do. Later, his wife Mary showed up and said, "He wants you." I went with her. He sat me in a corner, ignored me for a time, then finally said, "You're going to play in *Stagecoach*."

"This made me a star and I'll be grateful to him forever. But I don't think he ever really had any kind of respect for me as an actor until I made *Red River* for Howard Hawks, ten years later. Even then, I was never quite sure."

No major studio wanted to touch the story of *Stagecoach,* as the star was untried and the story, which concerned the journey of a stagecoach through Indian-infested territory, was considered too corny. At long last Walter Wanger, an independent producer, took a chance. The resulting picture won a number of high honors and made John Wayne a star, a name to be reckoned with at the box-office.

Ford bullied Wayne on the set of *Stagecoach* for two good reasons. First, he knew if he could arouse Wayne's anger, it would mobilize all his emotions and he would give a better performance. He wanted to help Wayne shake off the bad habits of ten years of mechanical acting in quickie Westerns. Secondly, he was afraid the other actors, who were all big stars, would resent the fact that Ford had placed one of his protegés in an important role. By taking the offensive against him, Ford suspected he could get the rest of the cast on Wayne's side. His tactics worked beautifully.

John Wayne at last had arrived. A major role in a big "A" Western, directed by the prestigeous John Ford. The critics joined in and proclaimed the birth of a new screen star. But not even the wildest publicity blurbs from the most exaggerating press-agent could predict the magnitude and longitude of the new star.

Wayne was still under contract to Republic and continued to make the Mesquiteer series and was loaned out to other studios. His first picture for RKO Radio Pictures was *Allegheny Uprising*, an early American Western. The first fully "A" Western produced by Republic was *The Dark Command*, which reunited him with Raoul Walsh, who had directed him in *The Big Trail* some ten years earlier. Unlike *The Big Trail*, this picture was very successful and one of the best Westerns Wayne made in the 'forties. Appearing with him was Roy Rogers, who later was to become the star of the singing cowboys at Republic, taking some of Wayne's thunder as a Western star but never rivaling him in popularity.

Wayne's first color feature was *Shepherd of the Hills* for Paramount, which was successful for the studio and for Wayne. Between loan-outs to other studios, Wayne continued to make features for Republic: *A Man Betrayed* and *Lady From Louisiana*.

In 1942, Cecil B. DeMille, Granddaddy of Spectacle and a star-maker second to none, cast John Wayne in a rip-roaring sea epic called *Reap the Wild Wind*. This film drew audiences who didn't visit the usual action dramas, Westerns or war epics, but could be drawn to a DeMille extravagance. The climb to Number One position was growing nearer.

With the war in full swing, Wayne made the first of his war films, of which in later years the gagsters would remark, "How could we have won the war without John Wayne?" Though he only made five pictures on the war during the war years (*Flying Tigers, Reunion in France, Fighting Sea-bees, Back to Bataan, They Were Expendable*) he is the war hero we most remember. And it wasn't until after the war that he made the best of the Wayne war movies: *Sands of Iwo Jima,* which earned him an Oscar nomination.

In 1947, John Wayne became the producer of his own films with *The Angel and the Badman,* a well-acted, well-made Western. Wayne proudly noted that all his Westerns have made money. Practically everything he's ever done has made money.

In that same year Wayne began the final climb to the very rarefied atmosphere of star, then super-star and finally—legend. Starting with *Fort Apache* and running through *Wake of the Red Witch, Red River, 3 Godfathers, She Wore a Yellow Ribbon, Sands of Iwo Jima,* and *Rio Grande,* John Wayne became the number one box-office star. And he has been listed among the Hollywood's top ten list for sixteen consecutive years since.

Not only was he favored at the box-office, but the critics began to notice that Wayne could act. Under the Svengali-like direction of John Ford, a very different Wayne emerged. An actor with more depth to his characterizations. The critics began to tell the audience what they had known for years, that Wayne was an important screen personality, or more precisely "a screen presence," the stuff super-stars are made of.

A movie exhibitor was once quoted as stating, "Put John Wayne's name on a newsreel and it will do business." On May 8, 1949, after starring in twenty-nine pictures, and playing the lead in about sixty quickie Westerns during twenty-two years in Hollywood, John Wayne suddenly found himself a big box-office click at forty-one, with eight movies playing simultaneously over the country (*Fort Apache, Wake of the Red Witch, 3 Godfathers, Stagecoach, The Long Voyage Home, Dark Command, War of the Wildcats,* and *Doomed Battalion*). Five of those films were re-issues. There was

nothing wrong with the movie industry that couldn't be cured by a dozen John Wayne films.

The 1950's brought John Wayne a new wife, saw the close of Republic Pictures and three films for Howard Hughes.

Some twenty years after leaving Warner Brothers, Wayne returned to do *Operation Pacific* and eight more films for that studio over a period of five years. Among them were two of his best Westerns: *Hondo*, shot in 3-D but released in regular 35mm, and John Ford's *The Searchers*.

Starting with *Jet Pilot*, Wayne made three films for the mystery man of films, Howard Hughes. Begun in 1950, *Jet Pilot* was finally released in 1957. In between, Wayne made *Flying Leathernecks* and *The Conqueror*, which had the most stilted dialogue of any Wayne film since talkies began. Nevertheless, *The Conqueror* was an action-packed, money-making movie, John Wayne lording over all as Genghis Khan.

The last picture Wayne made for Republic was *The Quiet Man* in 1952. Coming to Republic, almost at its birth, Wayne was to spend more than fifteen years with them, and to remark years later, "We grew up together."

About this time John Wayne married for the third time. His first wife was Josephine Saenz. She and Wayne had four children. They were divorced in 1946, and that same year Wayne married a pepper-pot Mexican actress, Esperanza Baur. His life with "Chata" was chaotic. Their passionate, ultimately unhappy marriage ended in 1953 in a public divorce hearing. His third marriage in 1954 has been the happy one. Pilar Pallette Wayne is the daughter of a Peruvian senator. She is a woman of classic calm and beauty, a friend and confidante of all Wayne's children and the mother of their daughter Aissa.

Beginning with his first scene in *Stagecoach* and running through the next thirty years to the final scene in *True Grit*, the freeze frame close-up of old, battered Rooster Cogburn, John Wayne became legend.

John Wayne's screen presence has fused into a legend, the man and the myth are one. Tall in the saddle, strong and silent, the traditional American Western hero, the inexorable force behind a soft, slow voice; sex attraction submerged by a reverence

for good women; cunning and ruthless in the cause of right, he embodies the lore of what people, especially those who prefer the illusion to the realities of history, like to think of as the Old West. The frontier is gone, but John Wayne remains, like the Statue of Liberty, or the Alamo, an American landmark.

John Wayne, the Big Daddy of all he-man Western stars. "I've been around movies long enough for millions of people to have been born, have kids and die. But *I'm* still working." Since 1929 Wayne hasn't once been off a studio payroll.

In 1960, John Wayne was producer, director and star of his own Batjac production of *The Alamo*. Costing twelve million dollars, it lost heavily and cost Wayne much of his personal fortune. Wayne freely admitted that he was in hock for *The Alamo*. He owned all of, or part of, hotels, cotton plantations, oil wells, real estate. All of it rode on *The Alamo*.

On the verge of total bankruptcy, Wayne, fifty-two and aging, started to grind out more Westerns: *North to Alaska, The Comancheros, The Man Who Shot Liberty Valance, How the West Was Won, McLintock, Circus World*. They all made money and life started to look a little rosier.

In 1964, four-pack-a-day, chain-smoking, human chimney, John Wayne began to feel the effects of four decades of nicotine and tar. The cancer was located and after a successful operation at Good Samaritan Hospital, Wayne returned with the greater part of one lung removed, but with an even greater zest for life. "I licked the big C," was the closing line to the real life death-struggle.

In no time at all, the seemingly indestructible Duke was back in his cowboy outfit and making Westerns: *The Sons of Katie Elder, El Dorado, The War Wagon*.

In 1968, John Wayne again undertook to direct his own picture, *The Green Berets*. His film was the only movie made in the 1960's by a major studio that dealt with the most explosive subject of the '60's—Vietnam. Strongly pro-Vietnam and pro-American, the picture was venomously attacked by the film critics who reviewed the war and not the film. But the critics still haven't learned that reviewing a Wayne film is really pointless. Good, bad or indifferent, the paying public lines up to see the star

whole families grew up with. The picture was one of the biggest grossers for Warner Brothers in several years.

Hellfighters was seen and quickly forgotten. Then along came *True Grit*. The film critics were falling over each other in their praise of John Wayne and the film *True Grit*.

John Wayne, same big, broad-shouldered, gangling figure, same mannerisms, same voice and rolling gait. John Wayne, sixty years old, minus one lung, often finding breathing so difficult that an oxygen mask is kept alongside his chair during the shooting of a picture. Is this the portrait of a fallen idol? Hardly, they are just the facts that no make-up's artistry can hide. The hair is almost all gone, the face is leathery, the nose more prominent than ever. But on the silver screen, sixty feet tall and stereophonic, he assumes his rightful proportions, as super-star and the last cowboy hero.

Up on that big screen he is a living anachronism, but to see him in his cowboy outfit: the old sweat-stained brown stetson, the double-breasted blue flannel shirt and the tan leather vest, is like seeing Santa Claus. He is there, giving his present of one or two Wayne pictures, each and every year, stretching back to the dawn of memory of many now living. For all those years, even out of cowboy uniform, as a mariner or crimefighter, he is always *Duke*. As long as he can walk without crutches, scan the horizon with one good eye, and ride the horse into the sunset without falling off, John Wayne will be there at your local theatre, the first and last cowboy hero the majority of us will ever know.

John Wayne's Westerns are always made in color. In two colors to be exact: greenback green and glittering gold. He looms above the other Western heroes the way the heads on Mount Rushmore dominate the surrounding pebbles. He may be homely, middle-aged and battered, but he is *the* Western star.

Rooster Cogburn may be Wayne's best performance. Nominated for the second time by the Academy of Motion Picture Arts and Sciences for his performance in *True Grit*, this picture may turn out to be his swan song to Westerns. "It's sure as hell my first decent role in twenty years," Wayne said, "and my first chance to play a character role instead of John Wayne. Ordinarily they just stand me up there and run everybody up against me."

Even the "new wave" film critics, who idolize Chaplin, Keaton, Hitchcock, Hawks, Dietrich, Bogart, are beginning to be enchanted by the Wayne mystique. Starting overseas, where Americana is more quickly appreciated than on the home front, Wayne is called the main actor in the American morality play—the Western. He became the essence of the Western man, as remembered in film, novel and legend. He was kind to women tough to men; fearing neither man nor beast but only God and His next of kin, true to his word and fast with his gun.

In the necessary fantasies of the national collective mind, John Wayne is the High Priest of a morality play where the greater good outdraws the deeper evil and walks into the sunset bloodied but unvanquished.

"Don't ever," Wayne said, "make the mistake of looking down your nose at Westerns. They're art—the good ones, I mean. Sure, they're simple, but simplicity is art.

"They deal in life and sudden death and primitive struggle, and with basic emotions—love, hate, anger. In other words, they're made of the same raw materials Homer used. In Europe they understand that better than we do over here. They recognize their relationship to the old Greek stories that are classics now, and they love 'em. But I don't think that's the reason they love 'em.

"We love 'em, too, but not because of anything we stop to think about. A horse is the greatest vehicle for action there is. Planes, automobiles, trains, they're great, but when it comes to getting the audience's heart going they can't touch a horse.

"He's basic, too. Put a man on him and you've got the makings of something magnificent—physical strength, speed where you can see and feel it, heroism.

"And the hero, he's big and strong. You pit another big strong man against him, with both their lives at stake, and there's a simplicity of conflict you can't beat.

"Maybe we don't tell it with poetry like Homer did, but in one way we've even got him beat. We never let Hector turn tail and run from Achilles. There's got to be a showdown.

"Westerns are folklore, just the same as *The Iliad* is. And folklore is international. Our Westerns have the same appeal in Germany and Japan and South America and Greece that they have in our country.

"But don't ever think they're foolproof, either. It takes good men to make good Westerns. And besides that, they're fun. I like making Westerns.

"We'll have Western pictures as long as the cameras keep turning. There may be periods when not enough good ones are made or when too many are made, but the fascination that the Old West has for Americans—for that matter, for the people all around the world—will never die out.

"Each new generation discovers it. There's no reason to expect human nature to change, so this situation is going to continue. And I'll keep on making them until I stop acting."

John Wayne doesn't play the hero in the Sir Galahad style, 100 percent pure. John plays the man who lives by a code. A sympathetic character, but whether good or bad depends on the point of view.

As John Wayne describes him: "He's a man of his place and time, and maybe a victim of circumstance or past mistakes. But he's living by a moral code of his own, a code just as rigid in its fashion as the ones on the books.

"Nobody says the end justifies the means or anything like that because it never does. And that's why I don't play heroes—good guys. I'm not what you'd call a villain, either. But one thing I make sure of—the guys I play are believable human beings.

"And if they don't exactly personify virtue, there's usually a pretty solid moral comment in the story."

In 1969 John Wayne celebrated his fortieth year in the motion picture industry. In 1970 the industry paid the highest tribute to its biggest box-office attraction. John Wayne, the Duke of Hollywood, was awarded the Oscar as Best Actor for his performance in *True Grit*. Nominated once before, in 1950 for *Sands of Iwo Jima,* the second time would have been the last time.

True Grit, based on a novel written with John Wayne in mind for the screen role, is a classic adventure story, and it was the parody of all past adventure films that Wayne or his imitators played in. The last hero exaggerated into self-parody yet emerging unvanquished and riding off into the winter sunset.

There is no denying the fact that John Wayne is but a shadow of his former self, the tall-in-the-saddle cowboy has become a crabby grandfather, playing the familiar role of John Wayne, Hero. The mountain of a man who endured forty years of riding and slugging across the silver screen, has started to crumble. The voice is gravel, the face fleshed out and the body portly. Watching the later Wayne, one begins to wonder what appeal is left in him that still fills theatres with paying viewers. It couldn't all be nostalgia or conditioned behavior. Perhaps it's the same old "screen presence" that kept him afloat on a sea of "B" Westerns and finally catapulted him to stardom. Or, that Wayne is so much part of the American folklore created by the moving picture, that to reject Wayne is to reject the American Dream. Or maybe it's simply that there's no movie like a good John Wayne movie.

For many years John Wayne walked through movies whose only function was to make money and provide entertainment no small accomplishment. Under the direction of a strong director like Ford, Hawks or Hathaway, Wayne is at his best.

On the set, he stands at mountain height, above everything except the overhead mikes. His hands shake noticeably. He is a big, big drinker, but he can still stand straight when his friends are stretched out, sleeping it off. "Sure I drink," Wayne says. "What about it? But I never indulge when I'm working. I've made several hundred rugged movies, and anybody who has worked so hard has *earned* a drink."

He is always there, where he is needed, with his lines memorized. He shows the other actors the little tricks—how to fall, for example. He kids around with the cast and the crew.

He is a careful and thorough worker. He knows how he wants to play his roles. He'll follow Ford's directions implicitly but isn't always that tractable with other directors. Wayne claims that regardless of the character he's portraying, "I'm John Wayne and that's who the audience wants to see."

Burt Kennedy, director of *War Wagon* was asked how he directed John Wayne. "How do you direct a legend? How do you structure a myth?" Ken-

nedy's answer is to let John Wayne direct himself.

John Ford seldom peruses a script without watching for a Wayne part, and conversely a call from Ford has special priority over Wayne's other commitments.

In characteristic mild rebuttal to assaults of critics upon his performances, John Wayne once said, "Nobody seems to like my acting but the people."

"My feeling about movie acting," Wayne continued, "is that it is like sitting in a room with somebody. The audience is with you—not like the stage, where they're looking at you—so you've got to be careful to project the right illusion.

"My advice to any actor who wants to work in outdoor pictures is to learn to fight. Learn to hit and learn to roll with a punch. Learn to handle your body easily and smoothly. You have to make it look good. Above all, it has to be convincing."

Wayne doesn't fret himself if he seems a little clumsy when he kisses the girl. "After all, a Western hero isn't supposed to be too adept in the love department. So if he fumbles, it doesn't make much difference. It's even better that way.

"But fighting is his business. That's where he has to be good."

For the last several years Wayne has been getting a million dollars per picture plus percentages, and he is the only actor who deserves it, and is worth the money. No Wayne movie ever lost money (all but his own produced and directed *The Alamo*).

As all big stars, Wayne cannot afford to sit brooding over scripts, waiting for a great one to come along before he makes a movie. That is the road to oblivion. Stars have a score of people revolving around them, whose livelihoods depend on the star making movies that make money. So Wayne continues with his two-films-a-year schedule, and will continue until his fans desert him or the old Duke is no more. It is hard to imagine a year passing without one new John Wayne movie playing at the local theatre.

After *True Grit*, Wayne continued on the Western trail with *The Undefeated* and *Chisum*. And the end is nowhere in sight.

Like all men of his age, Wayne has to go to funerals of his contemporaries and is forced to think occasionally of death. Returning from a funeral of a business associate of many years, Wayne remarked, "God, how I hate solemn funerals! When I die take me into a room and burn me. Then my family and a few friends should get together, have a few belts and talk about the crazy old times we had together."

Wayne is as rough and tough and as kind and gentle and as resourceful as any American who ever crossed the country in a covered wagon. I wonder if any of those men of the Old West could match him when it comes to guts or shooting a horse. This guy is a throwback to the old days.

The clue to Wayne is that he is by taste and by way of life, typical of the ruggedly individualistic nineteenth century frontiersman he portrays so persuasively. Like his screen image, he believes in Abe Lincoln, gallantry to women, a patriarchal family life and "rough, lusty wild guys who can change into heroes for the cause of liberty."

Wayne surrounds himself with tokens of American folklore. He has some of the most comprehensive private collections: paintings, sculpture and rare books on the American Indian and cowboy.

Here is a man who takes bigger risks in real life than does the one-dimensional screen image he portrays. "I'm not the sort to back away from a fight. I don't believe in shrinking from anything. It's not my speed. I'm a guy who meets adversities head on," remarked Wayne.

His discovery was inevitable. He had what the guys in central casting call "the natural look." That means he shot it out with the forces of evil; when he roamed the badlands in search of purity or when he rode triumphant into the sunset, he placed between image and audience a shadow of honest reality.

John Wayne is Hollywood's most misunderstood man and underestimated talent. In his forty years as Hollywood's most durable money-making star (total film grosses are estimated at 400 million dollars), he has shown only a few facets of his

volatile and complex personality. He is reputed to be a monumental drinker, a brawler with a flaring temper, and a docile giant who allows his hero, John Ford, to bully him mercilessly.

We can only touch upon John Wayne, the celluloid legend. The private Wayne is for his family and close friends. The public Wayne is for his countless fans, those living and those yet to be born. Each new generation will discover for itself a John Wayne film. By sheer number and popularity, there must be a Wayne film playing in some part of the world, every day of every year.

John Wayne: Feo, fuerte y formal*

Steven Zmijewsky
New York City
February 26, 1970

* John Wayne was quoted in the *Time* magazine cover story of August 8, 1969 as saying that he would like to be remembered in these words which, in Spanish, mean: "He was ugly, was strong and had dignity."

THE FILMS OF
JOHN WAYNE

Mother Machree

FOX FILM STUDIO

CAST:

Belle Bennett, Neil Hamilton, Victor McLaglen, Ted McNamara, Ethel Clayton, Constance Howard, Eulalie Jensen, William Platt, Philippe De Lacy, Pat Somerset, Jacques Rollens. (John Wayne an unbilled extra.)

CREDITS:

Directed by John Ford. Written by Gertrude Orr. Based on a story by Rita Johnson Young. Photographed by Chester Lyons. Edited by Katherine Hilliker and H. H. Caldwell. Released with tinted sequences, music, and synchronized sound effects.

SYNOPSIS:

An Irish mother in America gives up her son in the interests of his future, becomes a housekeeper and

Belle Bennett and Victor McLaglen

raises her employers' daughter. Years later, when this girl and her son fall in love, the boy and his mother are finally reunited.

Running time: 75 minutes
Release date: January 22, 1928

Hangman's House

FOX FILM STUDIO

CAST:

Victor McLaglen, June Collyer, Hobart Bosworth, Larry Kent, Earle Fox, Eric Mayne, Belle Stoddard, John Wayne.

CREDITS:

Directed by John Ford. Written by Marion Orth, from a story by Donn Byrne. Adapted by Philip Klein. Title writer: Malcolm Stuart Boylan. Photographed by George Schneiderman. Edited by Margaret V. Clancey.

June Collyer, Larry Kent, and Victor McLaglen

SYNOPSIS:

Victor McLaglen, an exile Irish patriot, risks his life by returning to Ireland and helping a young couple. John Wayne is an overenthusiastic spectator who smashes a picket fence.

Running time: 7 reels
Release date: May 13, 1928

Frank Albertson and John Wayne

Salute

FOX FILM STUDIO

CAST:

George O'Brien, Helen Chandler, Stepin Fetchit, William Janney, Frank Albertson, Joyce Compton, Lumsden Hare, David Butler, Rex Bell, John Breeden, Ward Bond, John Wayne.

CREDITS:

Directed by John Ford and David Butler. Screenplay by John Stone, from a story by Tristram Tuffer. Dialogue by James K. McGuiness. Photographed by Joseph H. August. Edited by Alex Troffey.

SYNOPSIS:

A familiar story of the football rivalry between Army and Navy. George O'Brien is the cadet with the brother at Annapolis, played by John Wayne.

Running time: 86 minutes
Release date: October 6, 1929

Words and Music

FOX FILM STUDIO

CAST:

Lois Moran, David Percy, Helen Twelvetrees, William Orlamond, Elizabeth Patterson, Duke Morrison (John Wayne), Frank Albertson, Tom Patricola, Bubbles Crowell, The Biltmore Quartette.

CREDITS:

Directed by James Tinling. Story by Frederick Hazlitt Brennan and Jack McEdward. Lyrics and music by Dave Stamper and Harlan Thompson, Con Conrad, Sidney D. Mitchell and Archie Gottler, and William Kernell.

SYNOPSIS:

Eight big songs and a hundred chorus girls in a story of two college rivals engaged in a furious competition for the love of the campus belle and also the $1,500 prize for the best musical comedy number written by a collegian.

Running time: 81 minutes
Release date: 1929

Lois Moran and John Wayne

Stuart Erwin, Warren Hymer, J. Farrell MacDonald and Kenneth MacKenna

Men Without Women

FOX FILM STUDIO

CAST:

Kenneth MacKenna, Frank Albertson, Paul Page, Pat Somerset, Walter McGrail, Stuart Erwin, Warren Hymer, J. Farrell McDonald, Roy Stewart, Warner Richmond, Harry Tenbrook, Ben Hendricks, Jr., John Wayne, Robert Parrish.

CREDITS:

Directed by John Ford. Written by Dudley Nichols, from a story by John Ford and James K. McGuiness. Photographed by Joseph H. August. Edited by Paul Weatherwax.

SYNOPSIS:

A story of a submarine damaged and trapped on the ocean floor with fourteen men aboard. At the last moment the crew is rescued in a tautly written climax. John Wayne is one of the submariners.

Running time: 77 minutes
Release date: February 2, 1930

COMMENT:

This film is historic, in that it brought together for the first time John Ford, screenwriter Dudley Nichols and cameraman Joseph H. August—the team which was to make many of Ford's finest films.

George O'Brien and John Wayne

CAST:

George O'Brien, Helen Chandler, Antonio Moreno, Noel Francis, Eddie Borden, Harry Cording, Roy Stewart, John Wayne.

CREDITS:

Directed by A. F. Erickson. Cameraman: Daniel B. Clark. Author: Kenneth B. Clark. Scenario by Elliott Lester. Dialogue by Donald Davis. Edited by Paul Weatherwax. Sound engineer: Harry Freericks.

SYNOPSIS:

The life and death struggle between two men of the great open spaces.

Running time: 55 minutes
Release date: June 22, 1930

Rough Romance

FOX FILM STUDIO

Cheer Up and Smile

FOX FILM STUDIO

Arthur Lake, Charles Judels, and Dixie Lee

CAST:

Arthur Lake, Dixie Lee, Olga Baclanova, Whispering Jack Smith, Johnny Arthur, Charles Judels, John Darrow, Sumner Getchell, Franklin Pangborn, Buddy Messinger, John Wayne.

CREDITS:

Directed by Sidney Lanfield. Cameraman: Joe Valentine. Author: Richard Cornell. Scenarist: Howard J. Green. Dialogue by Howard J. Green. Edited by Ralph Dietrich. Recording engineer: Al Bruzlin.

SYNOPSIS:

Heartaches and love affairs of youth are beautifully played by Arthur Lake and Dixie Lee in this comedy drama. There are a number of unexpected twists to the story. Baclanova is an alluring vamp trying to steal Arthur away from Dixie Lee.

Running time: 76 minutes
Release date: June 22, 1930

Marguerite Churchill and John Wayne

The Big Trail

FOX FILM STUDIO

John Wayne and Marguerite Churchill

CAST:

John Wayne, Marguerite Churchill, El Brendel,
Tully Marshall, Tyrone Power, Sr., David Rollins,
Frederick Burton, Russ Powell, Ward Bond, Marcia
Harris, Andy Shufford, Helen Parrish.

CREDITS:

Directed by Raoul Walsh. Cameramen: Lucien An-
droit, Arthur Edeson. Author: Hal G. Evarts. Scenario by Jack Peabody, Marie Boyle, Florence Postal.
Dialoguers: Same as above. Edited by Jack Denniss.
Recording engineers: George Leverett, Don Flick.

SYNOPSIS:

This was a story of the old Oregon trail, a nation in
exodus to the promised land of the West. The plot

itself is sparse, but the movie moves with such breathless sweep and with such smashing climaxes that the story is relatively unimportant. Highlights of the film include a buffalo hunt, the crossing of a swollen river, and an Indian attack.

Running time: 125 minutes
Release date: November 2, 1930

John Wayne, Marguerite Churchill, Helen Parrish, and David Rollins

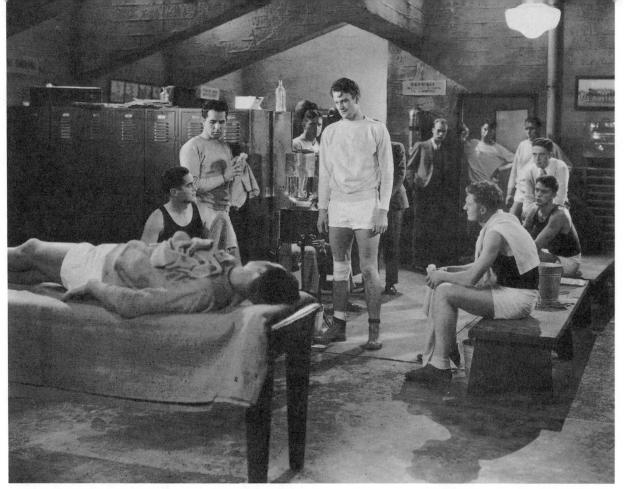

John Wayne and unidentified players

Girls Demand Excitement

FOX FILM STUDIO

CAST:

Virginia Cherrill, John Wayne, Marguerite Churchill, Helen Jerome Eddy, William Janney, Eddie Nugent, Terrance Ray, Marion Byron, Martha Sleeper, Addie McPhail, Ray Cooke.

CREDITS:

Directed by Seymour Felix. Written by Harlan Thompson. Photographed by Charles Clarke. Edited by Jack Murray.

SYNOPSIS:

There is "war" between the girls and boys at a co-ed institution, with the males endeavoring to oust the females. John Wayne is the leader of the boys.

Running time: 79 minutes
Release date: February 8, 1931

Joan Marsh and John Wayne

Three Girls Lost

FOX FILM STUDIOS

CAST:

Loretta Young, John Wayne, Lew Cody, Joyce Compton, Joan Marsh, Katherine Clare Ward, Paul Fix, Bert Roach.

CREDITS:

Directed by Sidney Lanfield. Written by Robert D. Andrews. Scenario and Dialogue by Bradley King. Editor: Ralph Dietrich. Cameraman: L. William O'Connell.

SYNOPSIS:

Three girls come to the city to seek their fame and fortune. One is a good girl, one is a bad girl, and the other girl isn't too sure what she is really like. Loretta Young and Joan Marsh aren't given too much of a story but they do their best to keep the action going. Lew Cody is great as a racketeer, John Wayne not so good.

Running time: 80 minutes
Release date: April 19, 1931

Laura LaPlante and John Wayne

Men Are Like That

("ARIZONA")

COLUMBIA PICTURES

CAST:

John Wayne, Laura LaPlante, June Clyde, Forrest Stanley, Nena Quartaro, Susan Fleming, Loretta Sayers, Hugh Cummings.

CREDITS:

Directed by George B. Seitz. Written by Augustus Thomas. Screenplay by Robert Riskin and Dorothy Howell. Photographed by Teddy Tetzlaff. Edited by Gene Milford.

SYNOPSIS:

John Wayne is the hero, who breaks off with his girl upon his graduation from West Point, only to be transferred to an army post in Arizona where he again meets the girl, now married to John's commanding officer and best friend.

Running time: 67 minutes
Release date: October 16, 1931

39

John Wayne and Buck Jones

Range Feud

COLUMBIA PICTURES

CAST:

Buck Jones, John Wayne, Susan Fleming, Ed Le Saint, William Walling, Wallace MacDonald, Harry Woods.

CREDITS:

Directed by D. Ross Lederman. Written by Milton Krims. Photographed by Ben Kline. Edited by Maurice Wright.

SYNOPSIS:

Buck Jones is the sheriff who is called upon to arrest his friend. John Wayne is the son of the rancher accused of killing a rival rancher over a feud involving cattle rustling. Jones uncovers the real murderer at the scene of a lynching.

Running time: 64 minutes
Release date: November 22, 1931

Richard Cromwell, Joan Marsh, and Jack Holt

Maker of Men

COLUMBIA PICTURES

CAST:

Jack Holt, Richard Cromwell, Joan Marsh, Robert Allen, John Wayne, Walter Catlett, Natalie Moorhead, Ethel Wales, Richard Tucker, Mike McKay.

CREDITS:

Directed by Edward Sedgwick. Written by Howard J. Green and Edward Sedgwick. Photographed by L. William O'Connell. Edited by Gene Milford.

SYNOPSIS:

Jack Holt is the football coach of a university that's been losing for two seasons. He forces his son, Richard Cromwell, to play on the team. In the crucial game, the son's poor playing brings defeat. Cromwell goes to a rival college and wins the game from his dad's team. John Wayne is a college football player.

Running time: 71 minutes
Release date: December 24, 1931

Harry Woods and John Wayne

Haunted Gold

WARNER BROS.

CAST:

John Wayne, Sheila Terry, Erville Alderson, Harry Woods, Otto Hoffman, Martha Mattox, Blue Washington.

CREDITS:

Produced by Leon Schlesinger. Directed by Mack V. Wright. Written by Adele Buffington. Photographed by Nick Musuraca. Edited by William Clemens.

SYNOPSIS:

John Wayne and Sheila Terry battle an outlaw gang for an abandoned gold mine. A mysterious figure called The Phantom haunts the gold mine, and in the end it is discovered he is Sheila Terry's father. He has amassed a fortune in gold since his release from prison, and only Wayne's arrival in the nick of time prevents the outlaws from stealing the gold.

Running time: 58 minutes
Release date: January 11, 1932

Shadow of the Eagle

MASCOT PICTURE CORPORATION

CAST:

John Wayne, Dorothy Gulliver, Edward Hearn, Richard Tucker, Lloyd Whitlock, Walter Miller, Edmund Burns, Pat O'Malley, Little Billy, Ivan Linow, James Bradbury, Jr., Ernie S. Adams, Roy D'Arcy, Bud Osborne, Yakima Canutt.

CREDITS:

Supervised by Nat Levine. Directed by Ford Beebe. Story by Ford Beebe, Colbert Clark and Wyndham Gittens. Photographed by Ben Kline and Victor Scheurich. Edited by Ray Snyder. Sound by George Lowerre.

SYNOPSIS:

Nathan Gregory (Edward Hearn), owner of a traveling carnival is accused of being the Eagle, an unknown criminal who has been sending mysterious threats to the officers of a large corporation by skywriting. Gregory, known as the Eagle for his sensational flying in the war, denies the charges although he admits a motive for revenge in the fact that the success of the corporation is due to an invention stolen from him.

Craig McCoy (John Wayne), one of Gregory's troupe, is also a clever sky-writer and pilot. Craig discovers the plans of the invention stolen from Gregory's trunk, and he pursues Green (Lloyd Whitlock), a director of the corporation, who is running from the scene. Craig gives chase and follows him to a telephone booth and hears him call a director's meeting for that night.

Back on the circus grounds, Craig and Jean (Dorothy Gulliver), Gregory's daughter, discover that Gregory has disappeared. Craig crashes the meeting that night, but is unable to convince the directors of Gregory's innocence. An airplane motor is heard. As they watch the plane, it writes the name Clark, then draws a line through it. The lights go out, a hollow voice proclaims that the Eagle has struck. A shot rings out and Clark is murdered.

Craig returns to the carnival where Jean receives a note from her father. Pinpoints on certain letters on the note show him to be a prisoner. Craig finds out where Gregory is held, and in the final chapter the Eagle is unmasked, but not before many thrills and spills.

Running time: Twelve chapters
Release date: 1932

John Wayne and Walter Miller

Hurricane Express

MASCOT PICTURE CORPORATION

CAST:

John Wayne, Shirley Grey, Tully Marshall, Conway Tearle, J. Farrell MacDonald, Matthew Betz, James Burtis, Lloyd Whitlock, Edmund Breese, Al Bridge, Ernie Adams, Charles King, Glenn Strange.

CREDITS:

Supervised by Nat Levine. Directed by Armand Schaefer and J. P. McGowan. Story by Colbert Clark, Barney Sarecky and Wyndham Gittens. Adaptation and dialogue by Wyndham Gittens, Colbert Clark,

Barney Sarecky, Harold Tarshin, George Morgan and J. P. McGowan. Photographed by Ernest Miller and Carl Wester. Edited by Ray Snyder. Sound by George Lowerre.

SYNOPSIS:

This is a railroad story of Larry Baker (John Wayne), a young air transport pilot whose father is killed in one of a series of mysterious train wrecks, and the hair-raising situations which result when he begins to track down and demolish the Wrecker.

Rivalry between the L&R railroad and the air transport line is keen and Gray (Lloyd Whitlock), the head of the airline, is under suspicion. But, so is Stratton (Edmund Breese), an escaped convict who had been falsely prosecuted by an official of the L&R for embezzlement. Then, too, there's Jordan (Matthew Betz), a discharged employee, who vows to get even. And Gloria (Shirley Grey), Stratton's daughter whom Larry loves is, for reasons of her own, working under an assumed name as secretary to the railroad manager. All these, and many others, have a score to settle with the L&R.

Apprehension of the Wrecker is complicated by his diabolical ability to assume the appearance of anyone he may choose. But Larry is persistent and through it all—railroad wrecks; an air transport night attack on the Hurricane Express as it roars over the rails carrying a huge shipment of gold, with Larry and Gloria trapped as it careens madly through space; the terrible explosion in the mine shaft—through it all Larry chases the Wrecker. Finally in the twelfth chapter, the Wrecker is unmasked.

Running time: 12 chapters
Release date: 1932

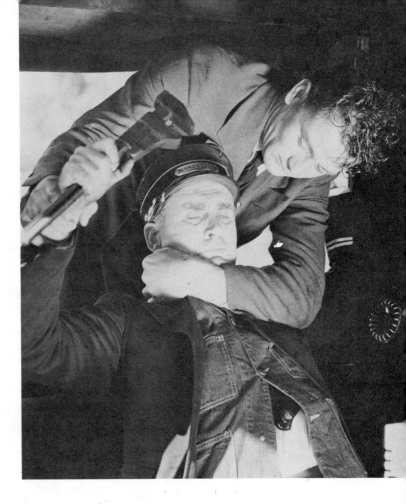

Tim McCoy, Shirley Grey, and John Wayne

Texas Cyclone

COLUMBIA PICTURES

CAST:

Tim McCoy, Shirley Grey, John Wayne, Wheeler Oakman, Wallace MacDonald, Harry Cording, Vernon Dent, Walter Brennan, Mary Gordon.

CREDITS:

Directed by D. Ross Lederman. Written by William Colt MacDonald. Dialogue by Randall Faye. Photographed by Benjamin Kline. Edited by Otto Meyer.

SYNOPSIS:

Tim McCoy is a Texas cowboy who rides into a strange town called Stampede. He is mistaken for a rancher who disappeared five years before, and who is thought dead. A head wound at the end restores the hero's memory of the past, and proves him to be the missing rancher and the girl's husband.

Running time: 63 minutes
Release date: July 8, 1932

John Wayne and Tim McCoy

Lady and Gent

PARAMOUNT PICTURES

George Bancroft and John Wayne

CAST:

George Bancroft, Wynne Gibson, Charles Starrett, James Gleason, John Wayne, Joyce Compton, Charles Grapewin, Frank McGlynn, Sr.

CREDITS:

Directed by Stephen Roberts. Written by Grover Jones and William Slavens McNutt. Photographed by Harry Fischbeck.

SYNOPSIS:

Bancroft and Gibson, as an ex-prizefighter and his nightclub singer girlfriend try to raise the orphan son of an old pal. John Wayne plays a young fighter.

Running time: 80 minutes
Release date: July 16, 1932

Two-Fisted Law

COLUMBIA PICTURES

cattleman, along with several other deals which had kept the community in a turmoil.

Running time: 64 minutes
Release date: August 30, 1932

CAST:

Tim McCoy, Alice Day, Wheeler Oakman, Tully Marshall, Wallace MacDonald, John Wayne, Walter Brennan, Richard Alexander.

CREDITS:

Directed by D. Ross Lederman. Written by William Colt MacDonald. Dialogue by Kurt Kempler. Photographed by Benjamin Kline. Edited by Otto Meyer.

SYNOPSIS:

Rancher Tim McCoy is cheated out of his ranch by a crooked cattleman. He finally pins the crime on the

Henry B. Walthall, Ruth Hall, and John Wayne

Ride Him, Cowboy

WARNER BROS.

CAST:

John Wayne, Ruth Hall, Henry B. Walthall, Harry Gribbon, Otis Harlan, Charles Sellon, Frank Hagney.

CREDITS:

Directed by Fred Allen. Written by Kenneth Perkins. Dialogue by Scott Mason. Film edited by William Clemens. Photographed by Ted McCord.

SYNOPSIS:

John Wayne comes to town in the days of the Vigilantes, and is in time to save Duke, the horse, from being shot on the charge of murdering a rancher. Wayne tames the horse, and with its aid succeeds in uncovering the real murderer.

Running time: 63 minutes
Release date: October 29, 1932

The Big Stampede

John Wayne and Noah Beery

WARNER BROS.

CAST:

John Wayne, Noah Beery, Mae Madison, Luis Alberni, Berton Churchill, Paul Hurst.

CREDITS:

Directed by Tenny Wright. Written by Marion Jackson. Dialogue by Kurt Kempler. Photographed by Ted McCord. Edited by Frank Ware.

SYNOPSIS:

In the early pioneer days, with a cattle rustling baron terrorizing the countryside, John Wayne is sent as a deputy sheriff to bring the baron and his gang to justice.

Running time: 63 minutes
Release date: November 11, 1932

The Telegraph Trail

WARNER BROS.

CAST:

John Wayne, Marceline Day, Frank McHugh, Otis Harlan, Yakima Canutt, Albert J. Smith, Clarence Gelbert.

CREDITS:

Directed by Tenny Wright. Written by Kurt Kempler. Photographed by Ted McCord. Edited by William Clemens.

SYNOPSIS:

John Wayne is a government scout who undertakes to get the supply train through to the camp of the men who are constructing the first telegraph line across the western plains.

Running time: 60 minutes
Release date: March 29, 1933

John Wayne, Frank McHugh, and Marceline Day

Richard Barthelmess

Central Airport

FIRST NATIONAL PICTURES

CAST:

Richard Barthelmess, Sally Eilers, Tom Brown, Glenda Farrell, Harold Huber, Grant Mitchell, James Murray, Claire McDowell, Willard Robertson, John Wayne.

CREDITS:

Directed by William A. Wellman. Author: Jack Moffitt. Adapted by Rian James and James Seymour. Editor: James Morley. Cameraman: Sid Hickox.

SYNOPSIS:

Because of an accident in which several of his passengers are killed, Richard Barthelmess, an expert pilot, is discharged. Later, he rescues Sally Eilers, a beautiful parachute jumper, whose chute was caught in a tree. When her pilot is killed, Barthelmess gets the job. Barthelmess and Eilers become sweethearts but he declares a pilot should never marry, and she is heartbroken. Barthelmess' younger brother, played by Tom Brown, also an aviator, meets Eilers and falls in love with her, and when Barthelmess is injured takes his place. Recovering, Barthelmess buys a wedding ring for Eilers but finds he is too late. She is already married to his brother. As a tramp flyer, Barthelmess wanders from country to country and becomes known as the world's greatest aviator. Eilers meets him accidentally in Havana and sees the wedding ring he had made into an amulet. When he explains, she confesses that she loves him best but a message comes that Tom Brown's plane is down in heavy seas, so Barthelmess takes his own plane and goes after Brown. He rescues his brother, says goodbye to Eilers, and returns to his wandering.

Running time: 70 minutes
Release date: March 29, 1933

John Wayne and Evalyn Knapp

His Private Secretary

SHOWMEN'S PICTURES

CAST:

John Wayne, Evalyn Knapp, Alec B. Francis, Natalie Kingston, Arthur Hoyt, Al St. John, Mickey Rentschler.

CREDITS:

Directed by Philip A. Whitman. Written by Lew Collins. Photographed by Abe Schultz. Edited by Bobby Ray.

SYNOPSIS:

John Wayne, as a rich man's son, can't take his mind off girls long enough to make a start in his father's business. He meets the granddaughter of a minister who eventually straightens him out and reunites him with his father.

Running time: 60 minutes
Release date: June 6, 1933

John Wayne, Evalyn Knapp, and Mickey Rentschler

John Wayne and Paul Fix

Somewhere in Sonora

WARNER BROS.

CAST:

John Wayne, Shirley Palmer, Henry B. Walthall, Paul Fix, Ann Faye, Billy Franey, Ralph Lewis, Frank Rice, J. P. McGowan.

CREDITS:

Directed by Mack V. Wright. Written by Will Levington Comfort. Dialogue by Joe Roach. Photographed by Ted McCord. Edited by William Clemens.

SYNOPSIS:

John Wayne is befriended by Walthall, and reciprocates by going to Sonora to look for Walthall's son who was shanghaied into a bandit gang. He finds the son and apprehends the gang.

Running time: 59 minutes
Release date: June 7, 1933

Life of Jimmy Dolan

WARNER BROS.

Lyle Talbot, Guy Kibbee, and Douglas Fairbanks, Jr.

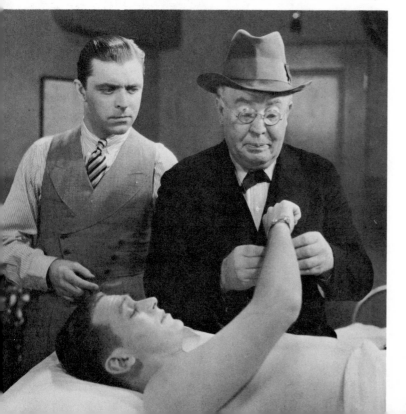

CAST:

Douglas Fairbanks, Jr., Loretta Young, Aline MacMahon, Guy Kibbee, Fifi D'Orsay, Shirley Grey, Lyle Talbot, Farina Harold Huber, George Meeker, David Durand, Dawn O'Day (Anne Shirley), Arthur Hohl, Mickey Rooney, John Wayne.

CREDITS:

Directed by Archie Mayo. Written by Bertram Milhauser and Beulah Marie Dix. Dialogue by Erwin Gelsey and David Boehm. Photographed by Arthur Edeson. Edited by Bert Levy.

SYNOPSIS:

Prizefighter Fairbanks, Jr. masquerades as his dead manager to avoid jail. He winds up in a sanatorium for crippled kids, becomes their idol, and risks capture to enter the ring again to pay off the mortgage. John Wayne has a bit part as a prizefighter. (This film later was remade as "They Made Me a Criminal" with John Garfield.)

Running time: 85 minutes
Release date: June 14, 1933

The Three Musketeers

MASCOT PICTURE CORPORATION

CAST:

John Wayne, Ruth Hall, Jack Mulhall, Raymond Hatton, Francis X. Bushman, Jr., Noah Beery, Jr., Creighton Chaney, Al Ferguson, Hooper Atchely, Edward Piel, George Magrill, Gordon DeMain, William Desmond, Robert Frazer, Emile Chautard, Robert Warwick, Rodney Hildebrandt, Wilbur Lucas.

CREDITS:

Supervised by Victor Zobel. Directed by Armand Schaefer and Colbert Clark. Story by Norman S. Hall, Colbert Clark, Wyndham Gittens and Barney Sarecky. Production manager: Larry Wickland. Photographed by Ernest Miller and Ed Lyons. Assistant cameramen: Monte Steadman and Joe Lykens. Dialogue by Ella Arnold. Assistant directors: George Webster and Louis Germonprez.

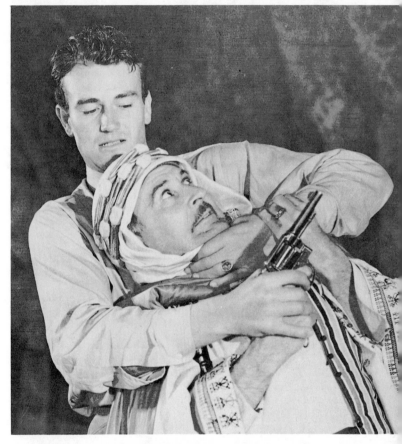

SYNOPSIS:

A supposedly updated version of Dumas' *Three Musketeers*, the latter-day D'Artagnan, Tom Wayne (John Wayne) and the latter-day Three Musketeers, Clancy (Jack Mulhall), Schmidt (Francis X. Bushman, Jr.) and Renard (Raymond Hatton), all Legionnaires in the deserts of Araby.

The Three Musketeers are rescued by the American D'Artagnan from certain death at the hands of desert rebels and followers of the mysterious El Shaitan. This evil figure, a man who never shows his face, a human vulture who plots death and destructive schemes, is hunted down by the Musketeers through twelve chapters until in the final chapter comes the unmasking.

Running time: Twelve chapters
Release date: 1933

John Wayne and Raymond Hatten

Barbara Stanwyck and John Wa[...]

Baby Face

WARNER BROS.

CAST:

Barbara Stanwyck, George Brent, Donald Cook, Margaret Lindsay, Henry Kolker, John Wayne, Douglass Dumbrille, Arthur Hohl, Theresa Harris, Harry Gribbon, Robert Barrat.

CREDITS:

Directed by Alfred E. Green. Written by Mark Canfield. Dialogue by Gene Markey and Kathryn Scola. Photographed by James Van Trees. Edited by Howard Bretherton.

SYNOPSIS:

Barbara Stanwyck, daughter of a disreputable speakeasy owner, decides to find her own way to success by using as stepping-stones a score of men, from department store managers to bank presidents. John Wayne has a bit-part as Jimmy McCoy.

Running time: 76 minutes
Release date: June 24, 1933

The Man from Monterey

WARNER BROS.

CAST:

John Wayne, Ruth Hall, Nena Quartaro, Luis Alberni, Francis Ford, Donald Reed, Lillian Leighton, Lafe McKee.

CREDITS

Directed by Mack V. Wright. Written by Leslie Mason. Photographed by Ted McCord.

SYNOPSIS:

John Wayne is a U.S. captain sent to Monterey to advise Mexican landholders to record their property under Spanish land grants or lose them to public domain. He uncovers double dealing, defeats the swindlers and saves the girl from marriage to the head scoundrel.

Running time: 59 minutes
Release date: August 16, 1933

John Wayne, Lafe McKee, Francis Ford, Ruth Hall, Nena Quartaro, and Donald Reed

Riders of Destiny

MONOGRAM PICTURES

CAST:

John Wayne, Cecilia Parker, George "Gabby" Hayes, Forrest Taylor, Al St. John, Heinie Conklin, Earl Dwire, Lafe McKee.

CREDITS:

Directed and written by Robert N. Bradbury.

SYNOPSIS:

John Wayne is an undercover secret service agent sent by Washington to help ranchers get water rights. He induces the gang leader to dynamite the well on the

John Wayne, George "Gabby" Hayes, and Cecilia Parker

girl's property, which releases water for the entire valley, and destroys his stranglehold on the water supply.

Running time: 50 minutes
Release date: November 24, 1933

Sagebrush Trail

MONOGRAM PICTURES

real killer. He befriends the real killer, who loses his life in a shoot-out with the bad guys.

Running time: 58 minutes
Release date: December 8, 1933

CAST:

John Wayne, Nancy Shubert, Lane Chandler, Yakima Canutt, Wally Wales, Art Mix, Robert Burns, Earl Dwire.

CREDITS:

Directed by Armand Schaefer. Written by Lindsley Parsons.

SYNOPSIS:

John Wayne is wrongly convicted for a killing. He escapes from prison and heads out West to find the

Lane Chandler, John Wayne, and Nancy Shubert

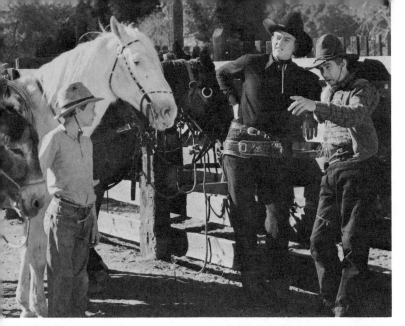

Billy O'Brien and John Wayne

West of the Divide

MONOGRAM PICTURES

CAST:

John Wayne, Virginia Brown Faire, Lloyd Whitlock, Yakima Canutt, George "Gabby" Hayes, Earl Dwire, Lafe McKee.

CREDITS:

Directed and written by Robert N. Bradbury. Photographed by A. J. Stout. Edited by Carl Pierson.

SYNOPSIS:

John Wayne returns to thè scene of his boyhood to find the murderer of his father, and to locate his little brother, missing since the murder. He saves the ranch, finds the murderer, wins the girl and finds his brother.

Running time: 54 minutes
Release date: January 13, 1933

Lucky Texan

MONOGRAM PICTURES

CAST:

John Wayne, Barbara Sheldon, George "Gabby" Hayes, Lloyd Whitlock, Yakima Canutt, Earl Dwire, Edward Parker.

CREDITS:

Directed and written by Robert N. Bradbury. Photographed by A. J. Stout. Edited by Carl Pierson.

SYNOPSIS:

John Wayne and "Gabby" Hayes discover a hidden streak of gold. Hayes is blamed for robbery and murder, but Wayne discovers it is the sheriff's son who is guilty.

Running time: 56 minutes
Release date: January 6, 1934

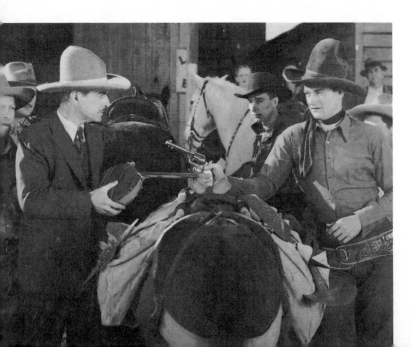

Blue Steel

MONOGRAM PICTURES

CAST:

John Wayne, Eleanor Hunt, George "Gabby" Hayes, Ed Peil, Yakima Canutt, George Cleveland, George Nash.

CREDITS:

Directed and written by Robert N. Bradbury. Photographed by A. J. Stout. Edited by Carl Pierson.

SYNOPSIS:

A band of outlaws plots to force the entire populace to quit a town, as there is gold in the soil. Wayne

John Wayne and Eleanor Hunt

convinces the townfolk to stay, encounters the outlaws, rescues Eleanor Hunt, and is revealed as a U.S. Marshal.

Running time: 59 minutes
Release date: May 5, 1934

The Man from Utah

MONOGRAM PICTURES

SYNOPSIS:

John Wayne is a deputy sheriff uncovering a gang who have made a racket out of the rodeo. Wayne enters the rodeo and exposes the gang.

Running time: 57 minutes
Release date: May 23, 1934

CAST:

John Wayne, Polly Ann Young, George "Gabby" Hayes, Yakima Canutt, Ed Peil, Anita Campillo, George Cleveland, Lafe McKee.

CREDITS:

Directed by Robert N. Bradbury. Written by Lindsley Parsons. Photographed by A. J. Stout. Edited by Carl Pierson.

John Wayne and George "Gabby" Hayes

Randy Rides Alone

MONOGRAM PICTURES

CAST:

John Wayne, Alberta Vaughn, George "Gabby" Hayes, Earl Dwire, Yakima Canutt, Tex Phelps, Arthur Ortega.

CREDITS:

Directed by Harry Fraser. Written by Lindsley Parsons.

SYNOPSIS:

John Wayne joins a gang to try to find out who has been robbing the local office of the express company. He rounds up the gang when he has all the evidence.

Running time: 60 minutes
Release date: June 14, 1934

John Wayne and Alberta Vaughn

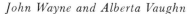

John Wayne and Alberta Vaughn

The Star Packer

MONOGRAM PICTURES

CAST:

John Wayne, Verna Hillie, George "Gabby" Hayes, Yakima Canutt, Earl Dwire, George Cleveland, Arthur Ortega, Edward Parker.

CREDITS:

Directed and written by Robert N. Bradbury. Photographed by A. J. Stout. Edited by Carl Pierson.

SYNOPSIS:

John Wayne rides into a town and organizes the ranchers who have been terrorized by The Shadow

Verna Hillie, Davie Aldrich,
Yakima Canutt, and John Wayne

and his gang. Wayne appoints the ranchers Deputy U.S. Marshals and cleans up the gang in a tough fight.

Running time: 60 minutes
Release date: July 3, 1934

The Trail Beyond

MONOGRAM PICTURES

CAST:

John Wayne, Verna Hillie, Noah Beery, Iris Lancaster, Noah Beery, Jr., Robert Fraser, Earl Dwire, Edward Parker.

CREDITS:

Directed by Robert N. Bradbury. Written by James Oliver Curwood. Screenplay by Lindsley Parsons. Photographed by A. J. Stout.

SYNOPSIS:

John Wayne is on a mission to the northwest to find a girl and a gold mine. He outwits a gang who are holding both the girl and the mine.

Running time: 55 minutes
Release date: September 15, 1934

Verna Hillie, Noah Beery, Jr., and John Wayne

Sheila Terry and John Wayne

'Neath Arizona Skies

MONOGRAM PICTURES

CAST:

John Wayne, Sheila Terry, Jay Wilsey, Yakima Canutt, Jack Rockwell, Shirley Ricketts, George "Gabby" Hayes.

CREDITS:

Produced by Paul Malvern. Directed by Harry Fraser. Written by B. R. Tuttle. Edited by Carl Pierson.

SYNOPSIS:

John Wayne is the guardian of a little Indian girl, the heiress of oil lands. He foils an outlaw gang who kidnap the girl, and blocks their attempts to kill her father.

Running time: 57 minutes
Release date: November 27, 1934

George "Gabby" Hayes, Sheila Terry, and John Wayne

Lawless Frontier

MONOGRAM PICTURES

CAST:

John Wayne, Sheila Terry, George "Gabby" Hayes, Earl Dwire, Yakima Canutt, Jack Rockwell, Gordon D. Woods.

CREDITS:

Directed and written by Robert N. Bradbury. Photographed by A. J. Stout. Edited by Carl Pierson.

SYNOPSIS:

The sheriff tries to pin some crimes on John Wayne, but Wayne is given a clean slate when the outlaw gang is rounded up.

Running time: 59 minutes
Release date: January 3, 1935

Sheila Terry and John Wayne

Earl Dwire, John Wayne,
George "Gabby" Hayes, and Jack Rockwell

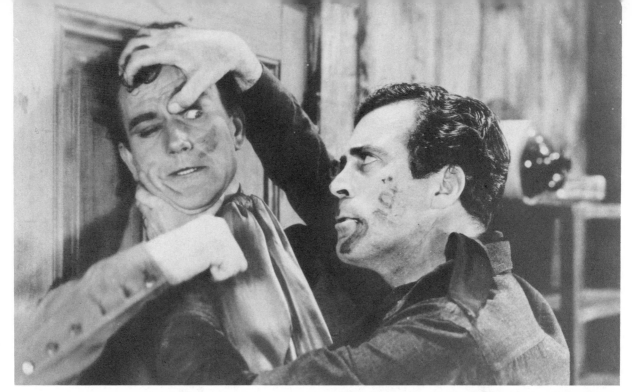

John Wayne and LeRoy Mason

Texas Terror

MONOGRAM: Distributed by Republic

CAST:

John Wayne, Lucille Browne, LeRoy Mason, George "Gabby" Hayes, Buffalo Bill, Jr., Bert Dillard, Lloyd Ingraham.

CREDITS:

Produced by Paul Malvern. Directed by Robert N. Bradbury. Written by R. N. Bradbury. Photographed by A. J. Stout. Edited by Carl Pierson.

SYNOPSIS:

Pursuing bandits, John Wayne believes he has killed his best friend by accident, when in reality LeRoy Mason is the murderer. Torn with anguish, Wayne seeks solitude in the lonely life of a prospector.

Lucille Browne, sister of the man Wayne thinks he killed, returns to the West and is attacked by bandits. Wayne rescues her and brings her to town safely. Later John finds a clue that leads him to the bandits and the man who killed his best friend. Fully exonerated, Wayne returns to the desert with Lucille to start a new life.

Running time: 51 minutes
Release date: February 1, 1935

John Wayne and George "Gabby" Hayes

Rainbow Valley

MONOGRAM PICTURES

Lloyd Ingraham (left) and John Wayne

CAST:

John Wayne, Lucille Browne, LeRoy Mason, George "Gabby" Hayes, Buffalo Bill, Jr., Bert Dillard, Lloyd Ingraham.

CREDITS:

Directed by Robert N. Bradbury. Written by Lindsley Parsons. Photographed by William Hyer. Edited by Carl Pierson.

SYNOPSIS:

John Wayne is an undercover agent sent to prison to get the goods on a gang through gaining the confidence of a fellow prisoner.

Running time: 52 minutes
Release date: March 12, 1935

George "Gabby" Hayes and John Wayne

Yakima Canutt (far left) and John Wayne (on ladder)

Paradise Canyon

John Wayne, Marion Burns, and Earle Hodgins

MONOGRAM PICTURES

CAST:

John Wayne, Marion Burns, Yakima Canutt, Reed Howes, Perry Murdock, Gino Corrado, Gordon Clifford.

CREDITS:

Produced by Paul Malvern. Directed by Carl Pierson. Written by Lindsley Parsons. Photographed by A. J. Stout. Edited by Gerald Roberts.

SYNOPSIS:

John Wayne is an undercover agent for the government sent to round up a gang of counterfeiters operating near the Mexican border. He lands the entire gang with the help of the Mexican *Rurales*.

Running time: 59 minutes
Release date: May 14, 1935

John Wayne and Marion Burns

The Dawn Rider

MONOGRAM PICTURES

CAST:

John Wayne, Marion Burns, Yakima Canutt, Reed Howes, Denny Meadows, Bert Dillard, Jack Jones.

CREDITS:

Produced by Paul Malvern. Directed and written by Robert N. Bradbury. Photographed by A. J. Stout. Edited by Carl Pierson.

SYNOPSIS:

John Wayne sees his father shot down in an express office holdup, and eventually brings the desperadoes to justice. Not before being shot, however, and nursed back to health by Marion Burns.

Running time: 56 minutes
Release date: July 9, 1935

Marion Burns and John Wayne

John Wayne and Sheila Manners

Westward Ho

REPUBLIC PICTURES

CAST:

John Wayne, Sheila Mannors, Frank McGlynn, Jr., Jack Curtis, Yakima Canutt, Mary McLaren, Dickie Jones, Hank Bell.

CREDITS:

Produced by Paul Malvern. Directed by Robert N. Bradbury. Written by Lindsley Parsons. Photographed by A. J. Stout. Edited by Carl Pierson.

SYNOPSIS:

John Wayne fights his brother, the brains behind the gang that killed their parents. Their kinship is revealed just as Wayne is facing death in a trap set by his brother.

Running time: 60 minutes
Release date: July 30, 1935

John Wayne and unidentified player

Edward Chandler, Mary Kornman, and John Wayne

Desert Trail

MONOGRAM PICTURES

John Wayne and Mary Kornman

CAST:

John Wayne, Mary Kornman, Paul Fix, Edward
Chandler, Lafe McKee, Henry Hull, Al Ferguson.

CREDITS:

Produced by Paul Malvern. Directed by Collin Lewis.
Written by Lindsley Parson. Photographed by A. J. Stout.

SYNOPSIS:

John Wayne, a star performer in a rodeo, clashes with
his friend over a girl, and brings holdup bandits to
justice. There are some good rodeo sequences.

Running time: 54 minutes
Release date: August 20, 1935

John Wayne and Edward Chandler

John Wayne, Muriel Evans, Murdock MacQuarrick and Mary McLaren

New Frontier

REPUBLIC PICTURES

CAST:

John Wayne, Muriel Evans, Mary McLaren, Murdock MacQuarrie, Warner Richmond, Sam Flint, Earl Dwire, Alfred Bridge.

CREDITS:

Produced by Paul Malvern. Directed by Carl Pierson. Written by Robert Emmett. Photographed by Gus Peterson. Edited by Gerald Roberts.

SYNOPSIS:

> WRONG!

The Mesquiteers help the ranchers fight for their land, which has been requisitioned to build a dam. They find their new homeland an Eden after the valley has been flooded.

Running time: 59 minutes
Release date: September 24, 1935

John Wayne and Muriel Evans

Duke is made sheriff and cleans up town after his father is shot in the back.

John Wayne and Sheila Manners

Lawless Range

A Trem Carr Production

REPUBLIC PICTURES

CAST:

John Wayne, Sheila Mannors, Earl Dwire, Frank McGlynn, Jr., Jack Curtis, Yakima Canutt, Wally Howe.

CREDITS:

Produced by Trem Carr. Supervised by Paul Malvern. Directed by Robert N. Bradbury. Original story and screenplay by Lindsley Parsons. Photographed by A. J. Stout. Edited by Carl Pierson.

SYNOPSIS:

John Wayne as an undercover agent is sent by the state governor to discover the motive behind the mysterious raids in the isolated Pequeno Valley. John finds the motive—gold mines—and stops the ruthless banker's attempt to drive out the inhabitants of the valley and keep the gold mines to himself.

Running time: 59 minutes
Release date: November 4, 1935

The Lawless Nineties

REPUBLIC PICTURES

CAST:

John Wayne, Ann Rutherford, Lane Chandler, Harry Woods, Snowflake, George "Gabby" Hayes, Etta McDaniel, Charles King, Sam Flint, Al Taylor, Cliff Lyons.

CREDITS:

Produced by Paul Malvern. Directed by Joseph Kane. Original story by Joseph Poland and Scott Pembroke. Screenplay by Joseph Poland. Photographed by William Nobles.

SYNOPSIS:

John Wayne, as an undercover government agent, is sent to break up a terrorizing gang. The finale is a pitched battle at the edge of the barricaded town and the clean-up of the gang and the capture of the leader.

Running time: 55 minutes
Release date: February 29, 1936

John Wayne and Ann Rutherford

John Wayne, unidentified players, and Cy Kendall (far right)

King of the Pecos

REPUBLIC PICTURES

CAST:

John Wayne, Muriel Evans, Cy Kendall, Jack Clifford, Frank Glendon, Herbert Heywood, Arthur Ayelsworth, John Beck, Mary McLaren, Bradley Metcalfe, Jr., Yakima Canutt.

CREDITS:

Supervised by Paul Malvern. Directed by Joseph Kane. Original story by Bernard McConville. Screenplay by Bernard McConville, Dorell McGowan and Stuart McGowan. Photographed by Jack Martin. Supervising Editor: Joseph H. Lewis.

SYNOPSIS:

Texas in the 1870's is an open cattle range, and a cattle baron, Stiles, has claimed most of it for himself. One homesteader refuses to move from his claim on the land, and he and his wife are murdered. Only the young son escapes. He grows to manhood, perfecting his marksmanship and lightning draw for the day of reckoning. He also studies law, and opens a law office in the heart of Stiles' territory.

The young lawyer, John Wayne, begins to challenge Stiles' claim to the land in the valley. In the final shoot-out Wayne is victorious and Stiles meets death when his wagon plunges off a cliff.

Running time: 54 minutes
Release date: March 16, 1936

John Wayne and unidentified players

The Oregon Trail

REPUBLIC PICTURES

CAST:

John Wayne, Ann Rutherford, Yakima Canutt, E. H. Calvert, Fern Emmett, Gino Corrado, Marian Farrell, Frank Rice, Joe Girard, Harry Harvey.

CREDITS:

Produced by Paul Malvern. Directed by Scott Pembroke. Written by Lindsley Parsons and Robert Emmett. Photographed by Gus Peterson. Edited by Carl Pierson.

SYNOPSIS:

John Wayne pursues renegade frontiersmen who lured his father into an ambush and forced his troopers to starve in the mountain snows. Wayne follows them, falls in love with Ann Rutherford en route, and with the help of Spanish soldiers defeats and captures the renegades.

Running time: 59 minutes
Release date: June 16, 1936

John Wayne and unidentified player

Winds of the Wasteland

REPUBLIC PICTURES

CAST:

John Wayne, Phyllis Fraser, Yakima Canutt, Lane Chandler, Sam Flint, Lew Kelly, Bob Kortman, Douglas Cosgrove, W. M. McCormick.

CREDITS:

Produced by Nat Levine. Directed by Mack V. Wright. Written by Joseph Poland. Photographed by William Nobles.

SYNOPSIS:

A tale of the changeover from pony express days to the stagecoach. John Wayne buys a stagecoach line and beats the rival stageline in a race to Sacramento for a $25,000 government mail contract.

Running time: 57 minutes
Release date: July 11, 1936

Unidentified players, Fuzzy Knight, and John Wayne

The Sea Spoilers

UNIVERSAL PICTURES

CAST:

John Wayne, Nan Grey, Fuzzy Knight, William Bakewell, Russell Hicks, George Irving, Lotus Long, Harry Worth.

CREDITS:

Produced by Trem Carr. Directed by Frank Strayer. Story by Dorrell and Stuart E. McGowan. Screenplay by George Waggner. Photographed by A. J. Stout and John P. Fulton.

SYNOPSIS:

John Wayne, a commander of a U.S. Coast Guard cutter, outwits and outfights a band of seal poachers and smugglers who have kidnaped his sweetheart, Nan Grey.

Running time: 63 minutes
Release date, October 24, 1936

Fuzzy Knight, John Wayne, and William Bakewell

73

Ann Rutherford, John Wayne, and Etta McDaniel

The Lonely Trail

REPUBLIC PICTURES

CAST:

John Wayne, Ann Rutherford, Cy Kendall, Snow-flake, Etta McDaniel, Bob Kortman, Sam Flint, Yakima Canutt, Bob Burns, Lloyd Ingraham.

CREDITS:

Produced by Nat Levine. Directed by Joseph Kane. Written by Bernard McConville. Photographed by William Nobles. Edited by Lester Orlebeck.

SYNOPSIS:

A tale of post-Civil War Texas, when the Carpet-baggers sought to exploit the South and her people. Gallant John Wayne helps the governor of Texas rid the state of Carpetbaggers.

Running time: 58 minutes
Release date: November 3, 1936

Jean Rogers and John Wayne

Conflict

UNIVERSAL PICTURES

CAST:

John Wayne, Jean Rogers, Tommy Bupp, Eddie Borden, Ward Bond, Harry Woods, Frank Sheridan, Bryant Washburn, Frank Hagney.

CREDITS:

Produced by Trem Carr. Directed by David Howard. Screenplay by Charles A. Logue and Walter Weems. Based on the Jack London story *The Abysmal Brute*. Photographed by A. J. Stout. Edited by Jack Ogilvie.

SYNOPSIS:

John Wayne is a lumberjack who is a member of a gang that conducts fake prizefights. He visits small towns, gains their confidence, then fleeces them. He meets Jean Rogers and decides to go straight, winning the fight and the girl.

Running time: 60 minutes.
Release date: November 28, 1936

John Wayne and Tommy Bupp

Tommy Bupp, Eddie Borden, and John Wayne

Louise Latimer and John Wayne

John Wayne and unidentified players

California Straight Ahead

UNIVERSAL PICTURES

CAST:

John Wayne, Louise Latimer, Robert McWade, Tully Marshall, Theodore Von Eltz, LeRoy Mason, Grace Goodall.

CREDITS:

Produced by Trem Carr. Directed by Arthur Lubin. Written by Herman Boxer. Photographed by Harry Neumann. Edited by Charles Craft and E. Horsley.

SYNOPSIS:

John Wayne wins a contest between his caravan of high-powered trucks and a special train. The contest is waged for delivery of aviation parts of rival manufacturers to a trans-Pacific liner before a labor strike takes place.

Running time: 67 minutes
Release date: April 16, 1937

Louise Latimer and John Wayne

John Wayne and unidentified players

John Wayne and unidentified players

I Cover the War

UNIVERSAL PICTURES

CAST:

John Wayne, Gwen Gaze, Don Barclay, James Bush, Pat Somerset, Charles Brokaw, Arthur Aylesworth, Earl Hodgins, Jack Mack.

CREDITS:

Produced by Trem Carr. Directed by Arthur Lubin. Screenplay by George Waggner. Photographed by Harry Neumann. Edited by Charles Craft.

John Wayne and Gwen Gaze

SYNOPSIS:

John Wayne, ace newsreel cameraman, is told by his boss, "Get the picture—we can't screen alibis!" Arriving at Samari, a desert hot-bed of tribal unrest and the home of El Kadar, bandit and rebel leader, John Wayne tries to locate and photograph El Kadar. John gets his pictures, but not before he has a romance with Gwen Gaze, a run-in with gun-runners, spies and throat-cutting tribesmen—and at the finale he saves the British Army.

Running time: 78 minutes
Release date: June 29, 1937

John Wayne and unidentified players

John Wayne and unidentified player

Idol of the Crowds

A Trem Carr Production

REALART PICTURES

CAST:

John Wayne, Sheila Bromley, Billy Burrud, Russell Gordon, Charles Brokaw, Virginia Brissac, Clem Bevans, George Lloyd.

CREDITS:

Produced by Paul Malvern. Directed by Arthur Lubin. Screenplay by George Waggner and Harold Buckley. Original story by George Waggner. Photographed by Harry Neumann. Edited by Charles Craft.

SYNOPSIS:

John Wayne joins a professional hockey team and helps them win. Just before the championship games, John is offered a bribe to throw the games. He refuses and an attempt is made on his life, which results in Bobby, the twelve-year-old mascot of the team, being seriously injured. During the second game John is injured but comes back strong and wins the championship and the girl.

Running time: 62 minutes
Release date: September 30, 1937

Sheila Bromley and John Wayne

Billy Burrud and John Wayne

Unidentified player and John Wayne

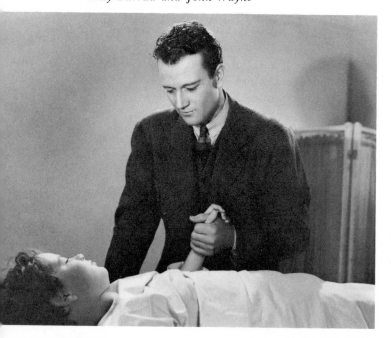

John Wayne and unidentified players

Adventure's End

UNIVERSAL PICTURES

CAST:

John Wayne, Diana Gibson, Moroni Olsen, Montague Love, Ben Carter, Maurice Black, George Cleveland, Glenn Strange, Britt Wood.

CREDITS:

Produced by Trem Carr. Directed by Arthur Lubin. Written by Ben Ames Williams. Photographed by Gus Peterson and John Fulton. Edited by Charles Craft.

SYNOPSIS:

John Wayne, a Pacific isle pearl diver, ships aboard a whaler. Before the voyage, the captain marries Wayne to his daughter as protection against the first mate. Together they face and survive the perils of a mutiny.

Running time: 68 minutes
Release date: November 11, 1937

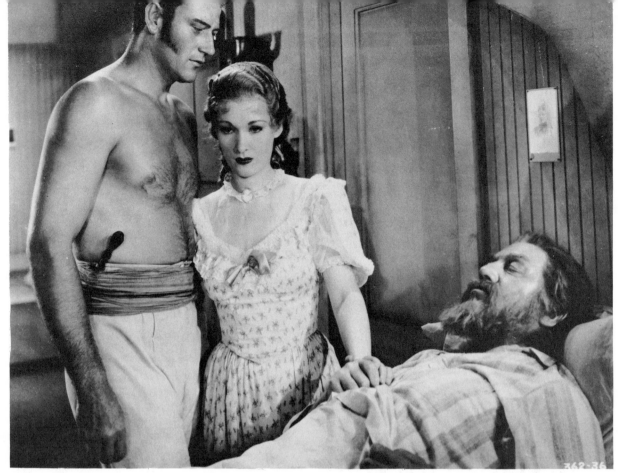

John Wayne, Diana Gibson, and Montague Love

Jimmie Lucas, John Wayne,
Moroni Olson, and Ben Carter

Jimmie Lucas, John Wayne, and Diana Gibson

Johnny Mack Brown, Marsha Hunt, and John Wayne

Born to the West

AKA Helltown

PARAMOUNT PICTURES

CAST:

John Wayne, Marsha Hunt, John Mack Brown, John
Patterson, Monte Blue, Lucien Littlefield, Alan Ladd,
James Craig, Nick Lukats.

CREDITS:

Directed by Charles Barton. Written by Zane Grey.
Photographed by J. D. Jennings. Edited by John Link.

SYNOPSIS:

John Wayne oversees a cattle drive and outwits rustlers, who later try to trim him in a crooked card
game. The cowhands arrive in the nick of time and
wipe out the rustlers.

Running time: 59 minutes
Release date: April 8, 1938

Marsha Hunt and John Wayne

Max Terhune, John Wayne, and Ray Corrigan

Pals of the Saddle

REPUBLIC PICTURES

CAST:

John Wayne, Ray Corrigan, Max Terhune, Doreen McKay, Frank Milan, Jack Kirk, Ted Adams, Harry Depp.

CREDITS:

Directed by George Sherman. Written by Stanley Roberts and Betty Burbridge. Photographed by Reggie Lanning. Edited by Tony Martinelli.

SYNOPSIS:

John Wayne becomes involved with a girl government agent getting evidence against a munitions ring who are shipping a rare chemical in its raw state, as salt, from a desert mine.

Running time: 60 minutes
Release date: September 15, 1938

Overland Stage Raiders

REPUBLIC PICTURES

CAST:

John Wayne, Louise Brooks, Ray Corrigan, Max Terhune, Fern Emmett, Frank LaRue, Anthony Marsh, Gordon Hart.

CREDITS:

Directed by George Sherman. Screenplay by Luci Ward. Photographed by William Nobles. Edited by Tony Martinelli.

SYNOPSIS:

The Mesquiteers buy an interest in the airport of an isolated gold mining town, then ship the gold by plane. John Wayne foils a band of hijackers and wins Louise Brooks.

Running time: 55 minutes
Release date: September 28, 1938

Unidentified player, Max Terhune, John Wayne, and Ray Corrigan

Santa Fe Stampede

REPUBLIC PICTURES

CAST:

John Wayne, June Martel, Ray Corrigan, Max Terhune, William Farnum, LeRoy Mason, Martin Spellman, Tom London.

CREDITS:

Associate producer: William Berke. Directed by George Sherman. Screenplay by Luci Ward and Betty Burbridge. Original story by Luci Ward. Based upon characters created by William Colt MacDonald. Photographed by Reggie Lanning. Edited by Tony Martinelli. Musical score by William Lava.

SYNOPSIS:

Farnum strikes gold and sends for the Three Mesquiteers, John Wayne, Ray Corrigan and Max Terhune. Mason tries to get the mine through unethical means and Farnum is killed. Wayne is accused of the murder, but the Mesquiteers find the real murderer and clear Wayne.

Running time: 58 minutes
Release date: December 8, 1938

Max Terhune, John Wayne, and Ray Corrigan

Max Terhune, John Wayne, and Ray Corrigan

Red River Range

REPUBLIC PICTURES

CAST:

John Wayne, Ray Corrigan, Max Terhune, Polly Moran, Kirby Grant, William Royale, Perry Ivins, Stanley Blystone, Lenore Bushman, Roger Williams, Olin Francis.

CREDITS:

Associate producer: William Berke. Directed by George Sherman. Original story by Luci Ward. Based on characters created by William Colt MacDonald. Screenplay by Stanley Roberts, Betty Burbridge and Luci Ward. Photographed by Jack Marta. Edited by Tony Martinelli. Musical score by William Lava.

SYNOPSIS:

The Three Mesquiteers are appointed special deputies by the governor in order to fight a band of rustlers in the Red River area. John Wayne disguises himself as an outlaw with a price on his head, joins the rustlers and gets evidence to bring them to justice.

Running time: 59 minutes
Release date: December 22, 1938

*John Carradine, Andy Devine, Chrispin Martin, George Bancroft, Louise Platt,
Donald Meek, Claire Trevor, John Wayne, and Barton Churchill*

Stagecoach

UNITED ARTISTS

CAST:

John Wayne, Claire Trevor, Thomas Mitchell, John Carradine, Andy Devine, Louise Platt, George Bancroft, Berton Churchill, Donald Meek, Tim Holt, Tom Tyler, Elvira Rios, Francis Ford, Marga Ann Deighton, Kent Odell, Yakima Canutt, Chief Big Tree, Florence Lake.

CREDITS:

Produced by Walter Wanger. Directed by John Ford. Screenplay by Dudley Nichols. From a story by Ernest Haycox. Photographed by Bert Glennon and Ray Binger. Art direction by Alexander Toluboff. Music by Richard Hageman, W. Franke Harling, John Lei-

John Ford and Tim Holt

pold, Leo Shuken and Louis Gruenberg. Edited by Dorothy Spencer and Walter Reynolds.

SYNOPSIS:

On the stagecoach from Tonto to Lordsburg, New Mexico, ride five passengers: Mrs. Lucy Mallory (Louise Platt), soon to become a mother, who is en route to join her Army officer husband at his frontier post; Mr. Peacock (Donald Meek), a timid-looking whiskey drummer; Doc Boone (Thomas Mitchell), a physician too fond of liquor; Hatfield (John Carradine), a mysterious gambler; and Dallas (Claire Trevor), a cafe dancer whom the ladies of the Law and Order League have forced to leave town. Bucky

Claire Trevor and John Wayne

Claire Trevor, John Wayne, Andy Devine, John Carradine,
Louise Platt, Thomas Mitchell, Barton Churchill, Donald Meek, and George Bancroft

(Andy Devine), the driver, shares his seat with Curley Wilcox (George Bancroft), U.S. Marshal.

Later, the Ringo Kid (John Wayne) gets aboard the stage, surrenders to Curly "until Lordsburg" where he is going to settle a feud. During the following hours, both outcasts, Dallas and the Kid, fall in love. At the first station stop, the group learns that Geronimo and his Apaches are on the warpath. Lucy collapses; Doc Boone, sobered by black coffee, delivers the baby with Dallas attending as nurse. Suddenly, Indian fires are seen, and Bucky makes the coach ready and drives on furiously. The stagecoach is soon surrounded by the redskins. In the intense battle that follows, Peacock is hit, Hatfield killed. At last, a cavalry troop arrives and drives the Indians off. Later in Lordsburg, Ringo shoots it out with his desperado enemies, and is wounded. Dallas rushes to him. Curley comes up with a buckboard, orders the two happy people to go on their way together to build a new life for themselves "across the border."

Running time: 96 minutes
Release date: February 15, 1939

George Bancroft, John Wayne, and Claire Trevor

Donald Meek, John Wayne, Andy Devine, Claire Trevor, George Bancroft, Louise Platt, Tim Holt, Francis Ford, John Carradine, Barton Churchill, and Thomas Mitchell

Unidentified players, Max Terhune, John Wayne, and Ray Corrigan

The Night Riders

REPUBLIC PICTURES

CAST:

John Wayne, Ray Corrigan, Max Terhune, Doreen McKay, Ruth Rogers, Tom Tyler, Kermit Maynard, George Douglas.

CREDITS:

Directed by George Sherman. Screenplay by Betty Burbridge and Stanley Roberts. Photographed by Jack Marta. Edited by Lester Orlebeck.

SYNOPSIS:

The Three Mesquiteers ride the trail in cape and mask to smash the cruel dictatorship of a cardsharp cheat who has risen to power over a vast area in the Southwest. In true Robin Hood fashion, the Three Mesquiteers clean up the situation.

Running time: 58 minutes
Release date April 4, 1939

John Wayne, Max Terhune, and Ray Corrigan

Three Texas Steers

REPUBLIC PICTURES

Ray Corrigan, Max Terhune, and John Wayne

CAST:

John Wayne, Carole Landis, Ray Corrigan, Ralph Graves, Max Terhune, Colette Lyons, Roscoe Ates, Lew Kelly, David Sharpe.

CREDITS:

Directed by George Sherman. Written by Betty Burbridge and Stanley Roberts. Photographed by Ernest Miller. Edited by Tony Martinelli.

SYNOPSIS:

John Wayne and the Mesquiteers come to the rescue of Carole Landis who has inherited a circus and a ranch in the Mesquite country. They win the stakes in a trotting race to pay off the mortgage.

Running time: 59 minutes
Release date: June 19, 1939

Raymond Hatton, John Wayne, and Ray Corrigan

Wyoming Outlaw

REPUBLIC PICTURES

CAST:

John Wayne, Adele Pearce (Pamela Blake), Ray Corrigan, Donald Barry, Raymond Hatton, LeRoy Mason, Yakima Canutt, Charles Middleton, Elmo Lincoln, David Sharpe.

CREDITS:

Directed by George Sherman. Written by Jack Natteford. Photographed by Reggie Lanning. Edited by Tony Martinelli.

SYNOPSIS:

The Mesquiteers show up a crooked local politician who has been selling state and federal jobs on road work to the impoverished ranchers.

Running time: 62 minutes
Release date: July 13, 1939

Ray Corrigan, Phyllis Isley (Jennifer Jones), and John Wayne

New Frontier

REPUBLIC PICTURES

CAST:

John Wayne, Ray Corrigan, Raymond Hatton, Phyllis Isley (Jennifer Jones), Eddy Walker, Sammy McKim, Leroy Mason, Harrison Greene, Dave O'Brien, Jack Ingram, Bud Osbourne.

CREDITS:

Associate producer: William Berke. Directed by George Sherman. Screenplay by Betty Burbridge, Luci Ward. Musical score: William Lava. Cameraman: Reggie Lanning. Editor: Tony Martinelli.

SYNOPSIS:

When the town of New Hope is condemned by the State legislature, the land to be used to increase the reservoir of a nearby city, the settlers defy the order. In a court test case, the State wins. With the settlers opposing the construction men and making it difficult for them to proceed with their work, the settlers are offered another piece of land and are promised that pipe will be laid to irrigate it. On the advice of the Mesquiteers the settlers accept this proposition. Later, however, they discover that the offer was fraudulent, but they succeed in saving the valley. The Mesquiteers ride again to save the settlers from the unscrupulous land grabbers.

Running time: 56 minutes
Release date: September 7, 1939

Allegheny Uprising

RKO RADIO PICTURES

CAST:

Claire Trevor, John Wayne, George Sanders, Brian Donlevy, Wilfrid Lawson, Robert Barrat, John F. Hamilton, Moroni Olsen, Eddie Quillan, Chill Wills, Ian Wolfe, Wallis Clark, Monte Montague, Eddy Walker, Olaf Hytten, Clay Clement.

CREDITS:

Produced by P. J. Wolfson. Directed by William Seiter. In Charge of Production: Pandro S. Berman. Screenplay by P. J. Wolfson. Based on the story *The First Rebel* by Neil Swanson. Photographed by Nicholas Musuraca, ASC. Edited by George Crone. Art direction by Van Nest Polglase. Assistant director: Kenneth Holmes.

SYNOPSIS:

Young Jim Smith (John Wayne) and other frontiersmen learn that Trader Callendar (Brian Donlevy) is supplying the Pennsylvania Indians with liquor and firearms. Janie McDougle (Claire Trevor) is in love with Jim, who is not the romantic type. He neglects courtship to go after a band of maurauding Indians, and then to Philadelphia to report the illegal traffic of the traders. Under the command of Captain Swanson (George Sanders), a force of British soldiers garrisons Fort Loudon to protect the settlers.

Callendar brings supplies to the fort, but also carries contraband for the Indians. Smith and his men, upon the refusal of Swanson to investigate Callendar's operations, disguise themselves as Indians and burn the wagon train. Upon Callendar's protests, Captain Swanson sends out soldiers to arrest Smith and his cronies. They manage to capture Janie, who has joined the raiding party. Smith and several of his men surround the military detachment and force Janie's release.

With reinforcements Swanson tries to take Jim and some of the ringleaders, but fails. The settlers go to the fort, demand a showdown in regard to Callendar, and being rebuffed, besiege the fort. Swanson capitulates and marches out with his men. Jim sends one of the trader's captured wagons to Governor Penn (Clay Clement) to prove what has been going on. Swanson returns with a larger force, reoccupies the fort and arrests many settlers. Jim and his friends recapture the fort. The prisoners are released and their shackles stricken off. However, some of Callendar's men kill a settler and cause Smith's arrest on the trumped up charge of murder. At a court martial Janie and the local magistrate dramatically demonstrate Jim's innocence, but before the trial ends a high-ranking British officer arrives and releases Jim and arrests his accusers. Swanson is sent back to England while Jim and Janie, re-united, set out for Tennessee.

Running time: 81 minutes
Release date: October 24, 1939

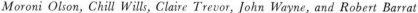

Moroni Olson, Chill Wills, Claire Trevor, John Wayne, and Robert Barrat

Roy Rogers, Claire Trevor, Walter Pidgeon, and John Wayne

Dark Command

REPUBLIC PICTURES

CAST:

John Wayne, Claire Trevor, Walter Pidgeon, Roy Rogers, George "Gabby" Hayes, Porter Hall, Marjorie Main.

CREDITS:

Associate producer: Sol C. Siegel. Directed by Raoul Walsh. Screenplay by Grover Jones, Lionel Houser and F. Hugh Herbert. Based on the novel by W. R. Burnett. Adaptation by Jan Fortune. Photographed by Jack Marta. Supervising editor: Murray Seldeen. Edited by William Morgan. Art direction by John Victor Mackay. Musical director: Victor Young.

SYNOPSIS:

In Lawrence, Kansas, before the Civil War, a schoolteacher, Will Cantrell (Walter Pidgeon), dreams of power. Cantrell tries for the office of Federal Marshal and he is embittered when cowboy Bob Seton (John Wayne) wins the election. He is even more embittered when he sees that Seton is making advances to Mary McCloud (Claire Trevor) whom he loves.

But when Mary's brother, Fletch (Roy Rogers), is tried for murder at Seton's lawful insistence, Cantrell sees his chance. Taking advantage of the resulting rift between Seton and the McClouds, he works his way into Mary's regard by threatening violence to the jury, so that they bring in a verdict of not guilty.

97

Intoxicated with his first taste of power, Cantrell organizes a band of guerillas who raid and pillage the countryside. Fletch McCloud, grateful to Cantrell for saving his life, joins the band of renegades. Furthermore, his distraught sister marries Cantrell.

Although Mary gradually comes to suspect Cantrell's infamy, she refuses to lose faith in her husband— until circumstances put Seton and herself in his grasp.

At last, in a ruthless attack on Lawrence in which innocent women and children are brutally murdered, Cantrell burns the entire city to the ground. Seton overpowers and kills Cantrell in a life-and-death struggle, and amidst the ruins of the pillaged city, Mary and Seton plan a new life together.

Running time: 92 minutes
Release date: April 5, 1940

Walter Pidgeon, Claire Trevor, and John Wayne

John Wayne, Claire Trevor, and Roy Rogers

*George "Gabby" Hayes
and John Wayne*

John Wayne and Walter Pidgeon

Sigrid Gurie, Charles Coburn, and John Wayne

Three Faces West

(Also called "The Refugee")

REPUBLIC PICTURES

CAST:

John Wayne, Sigrid Gurie, Charles Coburn, Spencer Charters, Helen MacKellar, Roland Varno, Sonny Bupp, Wade Boteler, Trevor Bardette, Russell Simpson, Charles Waldron, Wendell Niles.

CREDITS:

Associate producer: Sol C. Siegel. Directed by Bernard Vorhaus. Screenplay by F. Hugh Herbert, Joseph Moncure March and Samuel Ornitz. Production manager: Al Wilson. Photographed by John Alton. Edited by William Morgan. Supervising editor: Murray Seldeen. Art direction by John Victor MacKay. Musical score by Victor Young.

SYNOPSIS:

Dr. Karl Braun (Charles Coburn), famous Viennese surgeon of pre-Nazi days, arrives penniless in the U.S. with his beautiful daughter, Leni (Sigrid Gurie). They settle in Asheville Forks, a community in the heart of the Dust Bowl which is badly in need of a doctor.

John Phillips (John Wayne) falls in love with Leni but she is still in love with the ghost of Eric (Roland Varno), a young Austrian officer who had given his life to help her and her father escape from a concentration camp. Leni wants to leave Asheville Forks until her father becomes interested in a crippled boy and successfully operates upon him. Re-inspired by the happiness the successful operation produces in

100

John Wayne and Sigrid Gurie

the community, Leni decides to remain with her father and help him rehabilitate the people of the town. Later, as Eric's memory fades, she falls in love with John and they joyously plan to marry. Then she learns that Eric isn't dead after all, but is on his way to San Francisco to meet her, Leni feels duty-bound to marry Eric.

Repeated dust storms ravage the area and the whole community, under John's leadership, sets out for Oregon where workable tracts of land are available. Leni and John bid each other farewell, and the Brauns proceed to the coast to meet Eric. They find a new Eric, an Eric who wants to take Leni back to the Reich to reap the "benefits and glory of its conquests." This man means nothing to Leni and she no longer feels compelled to carry on their engagement. Happily she returns to John and they are married. Meanwhile Dr. Braun prepares to assume his medical duties to the newly located residents.

Running time: 79 minutes
Release date: June 14, 1940

John Wayne and Sigrid Gurie

John Wayne and Dewey Robinson

Jack Pennick, Thomas Mitchell, Ward Bond, John Wayne, and John Qualen

The Long Voyage Home

Argosy Productions

UNITED ARTISTS

CAST:

John Wayne, Thomas Mitchell, Ian Hunter, Barry Fitzgerald, Wilfrid Lawson, Mildred Natwick, John Qualen, Ward Bond, Arthur Shields, Joseph Sawyer, J. M. Kerrigan, Rafaela Ottiano, Carmen Morales, Douglas Walton, Billy Bevan, Cyril McLaglen.

CREDITS:

Produced by Walter Wanger. Directed by John Ford. Screenplay by Dudley Nichols, based on the play *The Long Voyage Home* by Eugene O'Neill. Photographed by Gregg Toland. Music: Richard Hageman.

SYNOPSIS:

Aboard the Glencairn off a Caribbean island, the crew's long-awaited party with native women ends in a free-for-all. Only Smitty (Ian Hunter) remains apart from the goings on. At Baltimore, the ship is dispatched for London with a cargo of dynamite; the men are nervous and disgruntled. Olson (John Wayne) dreams of returning to his home and family for good, and takes a lot of kidding from Driscoll (Thomas Mitchell), Yank (Ward Bond) and Cocky (Barry Fitzgerald), who secretly harbor the same dream.

In the war zone, a storm hits the ship and Yank is killed. Irritated by Smitty's strange behavior, the

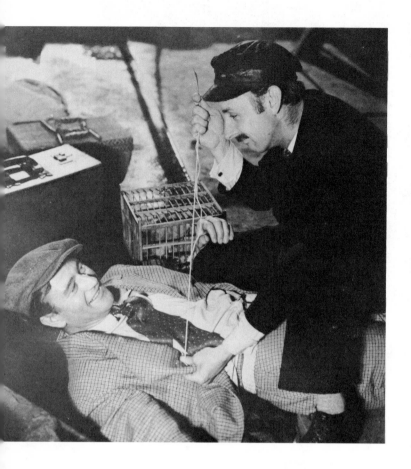

crew turns on him, accusing him of being a spy, only to discover that his brooding aloofness hides the heart-break of a wife who has left him because of his drinking. When enemy airplanes attack the ship, Smitty loses his life in a gallant effort to loosen a lifeboat. Finally landing in London, the crew makes for a pub. Only Olsen, with a rail ticket for home in his pocket, remains sober. A crimp, assigned to shanghai a man for a crew, dopes Olson's drink and drags him aboard the Amindra. When his pals learn of it, Driscoll leads them as they storm the ship, and in a terrific free-for-all, Olson is rescued. Driscoll, however, is knocked out, and is still aboard the Amindra as she sails. The next day, Olsen leaves for home; the rest of the sailors return to the Glencairn. They never see the newspaper headlines that report the torpedoing of the Amindra: with all hands, including Driscoll, lost.

Running time: 105 minutes
Release date: October 9, 1940

John Wayne and John Qualen

Thomas Mitchell, John Wayne, and unidentified girls

Marlene Dietrich and John Wayne

Seven Sinners

UNIVERSAL PICTURES

*John Wayne, Marlene Dietrich,
and unidentified players*

CAST:

Marlene Dietrich, John Wayne, Broderick Crawford, Mischa Auer, Albert Dekker, Billy Gilbert, Anna Lee, Oscar Homolka, Samuel S. Hinds, Reginald Denny, Vince Barnett, Herbert Rawlinson, James Craig, William Bakewell, Antonio Moreno, Russell Hicks, William Davidson, Richard Carle, Willie Fung.

CREDITS:

Produced by Joe Pasternak. Directed by Tay Garnett. Screenplay by John Meehan and Harry Tugend. Based on a story by Ladislaus Fodor and Lazlo Vadnal. Photographed by Rudolph Maté. Art direction by Jack Otterson. Musical director: Charles Previn. Sound by Bernard B. Brown. Music by Frank Skinner. Miss Dietrich's gowns by Irene. Costumes by Vera West.

SYNOPSIS:

Bijou (Marlene Dietrich), a honky-tonk singer playing the South Sea Island circuit goes to the American naval base at Boni-Komba with three cronies—Little Ned (Broderick Crawford), Sacha (Mischa Auer), and Dr. Martin (Albert Dekker). On the island, Tony (Billy Gilbert), proprietor of the Seven Sinners Cafe, gives the three jobs and it is here that Bijou meets Lt. Bruce Whitney (John Wayne). A fierce quarrel ensues when Bruce's superior officers try to force him to give up Bijou. Later, Bruce tells Bijou he has quit the navy. That night, Bijou returns to the cafe. Bruce tries to take her away and by pre-arranged signal with her, Little Ned starts a fight. Bruce is knocked out by Ned. Before he regains consciousness, Bijou leaves the island so that Bruce can go back to his true love—the navy.

Running time: 81 minutes
Release date: November 4, 1940

William Bakewell, Marlene Dietrich, John Wayne, and Broderick Crawford

Edward Ellis, Frances Dee, and John Wayne

A Man Betrayed

REPUBLIC PICTURES

CAST:

John Wayne, Frances Dee, Edward Ellis, Wallace Ford, Ward Bond, Harold Huber, Alexander Granach, Barnett Parker, Ed Stanley, Tim Ryan, Harry Hayden, Russell Hicks, Pierre Watkin, Ferris Taylor.

CREDITS:

Associate producer: Armand Schaefer. Directed by John H. Auer. Screenplay by Isabel Dawn. Original story by Jack Moffitt. Adaptation by Tom Kilpatrick. Production manager: Al Wilson. Photographed by Jack Marta. Supervising editor: Murray Seldon. Edited by Charles Craft. Art direction by John Victor Mackay. Musical director: Cy Feuer.

SYNOPSIS:

Lynn Hollister (John Wayne), a small-town lawyer comes to Temple City to investigate the mysterious death of his close friend Johnny Smith in a local night club, the Club Inferno. Smith was actually shot by Floyd Amato (Ward Bond), the moronic brother of T. Amato (Alexander Granach), proprietor of the Club Inferno—and one of Cameron's henchmen. Tom Cameron (Edward Ellis), political leader of Temple City, is an utterly ruthless politician, whose only soft spot is his affection for his beautiful daughter Sabra (Frances Dee).

Hollister, upon his arrival, goes straight to Cameron's residence. There he meets Sabra, who is attracted to him and invites him to escort her to the

Club Inferno. At the night club Hollister gains further evidence to support his conviction that Johnny was murdered and not a suicide as reported.

T. Amato becomes incensed over Cameron's failure to appoint him to a political office. Cameron decides to depose him. In revenge, Amato determines to defeat the Cameron machine in the coming election. He imports hundreds of inmates of local institutions for the poor, the feeble-minded, and the like, arranging for each one of them to vote several times. Hollister realizes that this feud offers him his long-awaited chance, and unearths an old law stating that any man suspected of voting illegally may be held without bail. When Cameron learns of Amato's plot to strip him of power, he imports a small army of racketeers to intimidate the "voters." In the ensuing fracas, Hollister corners Floyd Amato and forces him to confess that he was the one who shot Johnny Smith. Hollister invokes the illegal-vote law, and has the institution inmates and the racketeers rounded up and jailed. Several of them, outraged by what they consider a double-cross from the Cameron-Amato group turn state's evidence.

Running time: 83 minutes
Release date: March 14, 1941

John Wayne and Frances Dee

John Wayne and Ward Bond

John Wayne, Ona Munson, Helen Westley, Ray Middleton, and Henry Stephenson

Lady from Louisiana

REPUBLIC PICTURES

CAST:

John Wayne, Ona Munson, Ray Middleton, Henry Stephenson, Helen Westley, Jack Pennick, Dorothy Dandridge, Shimen Ruskin, Jacqueline Dalya, Paul Scardon, James H. MacNamara, James C. Morton, Maurice Costello.

CREDITS:

Associate producer-director: Bernard Vorhaus. Screenplay by Vera Caspary, Michael Hogan and Guy Endore. Original story by Edward James and Francis Faragoh. Photographed by Jack Marta. Edited by Edward Mann. Art direction by John Victor Mackay. Production manager: Al Wilson. Supervising editor: Murray Seldeen. Musical director: Cy Fever.

SYNOPSIS:

Julie Mirbeau (Ona Munson), a high-spirited southern belle, meets a young attorney, John Reynolds (John Wayne), on a Mississippi river boat, en route to New Orleans, and they fall deeply in love. When they reach New Orleans, John learns that Julie is the daughter of General Mirbeau (Henry Stephenson),

John Wayne and Ona Munson

owner of the lottery. Julie discovers that John is the lawyer engaged by the anti-lottery league to run the lottery out of town.

Blackie Williams (Ray Middleton), Mirbeau's first lieutenant, has designs on the general's daughter, and he fans the antagonism which develops between Julie and John. Julie, however, takes John to the Mardi Gras, in the hope of winning him over to the belief that the lottery is harmless. When one of the lottery winners is murdered by Cuffy (Jack Pennick), a Mirbeau gangster, John is determined that not even his love for Julie will blind his eyes to the evil influence of the lottery. He sets to work with a vengeance to expose the graft reaped by the Mirbeau machine.

General Mirbeau himself sincerely believes that large sums of lottery proceeds are being diverted to local hospitals, orphanages and levee-control equipment. When he discovers that Blackie has been keeping the money for himself, he dismisses him. Blackie retaliates by engaging some of his thugs to pose as reformers and to shoot Mirbeau. Just as Blackie has anticipated, Julie believes that John, as head of the reform element, is indirectly responsible for the murder of her father, but contrary to Blackie's plans, instead of marrying him and turning over control of the lottery to him, Julie takes personal charge of the enterprise.

Using her position as a lady of great charm to get into the good graces of the local public officials, she is able to thwart John at every turn. Julie is unaware of Blackie's methods, until John succeeds in gaining possession of the lottery records, incriminating all the public officials who have been protecting Blackie's racketeering. With this evidence, he rounds up all the lottery gang, including Julie. John assures Julie that he will do his utmost to help her; but she doubts his motives.

While John is presenting his testimony during the trial, a raging storm undermines the foundations of the courthouse and it has to be vacated. Blackie tries to escape with Julie, but as the levee gives way, he saves himself and leaves her on the levee to die. He secures passage on a steamer and bribes the captain to leave at once. John comes aboard the steamer and forces the captain to turn back and to use his boat to plug the break in the levee. In the ensuing battle, Blackie falls overboard and is drowned. The levee is saved; and after all the complications are cleared up, John claims Julie as his bride.

Running time: 84 minutes
Release date: April 22, 1941

John Wayne and Ona Munson

Betty Field, Tom Fadden, and John Wayne

The Shepherd of the Hills

PARAMOUNT PICTURES

CAST:

John Wayne, Betty Field, Harry Carey, Beulah Bondi, James Barton, Samuel S. Hinds, Marjorie Main, Ward Bond, Marc Lawrence, John Qualen, Fuzzy Knight, Tom Fadden.

CREDITS:

Produced by Jack Moss. Directed by Henry Hathaway. Screenplay by Grover Jones and Stuart Anthony. Original story by Harold Bell Wright, based on his novel *The Shepherd of the Hills*. Photographed by Charles Lang, ASC. Edited by Ellsworth Hoagland. Art direction by Hans Dreier and Roland Anderson. Color by Technicolor.

SYNOPSIS:

Young Matt (John Wayne), hot-headed mountaineer, vows to kill the man he believes wrecked his mother's life and placed a cloud over him since birth—his father.

Young Matt's relentless urge to wash away disgrace in blood is what keeps pretty Sammy Lane (Betty Field), his sweetheart, from marrying him. Young Matt learns that his father is the stranger who is called The Shepherd of the Hills by the mountainfolk because of his many kindnesses to them. In a dramatic climax The Shepherd (Harry Carey) comes to grips with his son and clears the way for Young Matt to live in happiness with his mountain sweetheart.

Running time: 97 minutes
Release date: June 18, 1941

Harry Carey and John Wayne

John Wayne, Joan Blondell, and chorus

Lady for a Night

REPUBLIC PICTURES

CAST:

Joan Blondell, John Wayne, Ray Middleton, Philip Merivale, Blanche Yurba, Edith Barrett, Leonid Kinskey, Hattie Noel, Montague Love, Carmel Myers, Dorothy Burgess, Guy Usher, Ivan Miller, Patricia Knox, Lew Payton, Marylin Hare, Dewey Robinson.

CREDITS:

Associate producer: Albert J. Cohen. Directed by Leigh Jason. Screenplay by Isabel Dawn and Boyce DeGaw. Based on a story by Garrett Fort. Photo-graphed by Norbert Brodine. Supervising editor: Murray Seldeen. Edited by Ernest Nims. Art direction by John Victor Mackey. Music by David Buttolph.

SYNOPSIS:

Memphis society rebels against the election of Jenny Blake (Joan Blondell), young and beautiful owner of a gambling boat on the Mississippi, as Queen of the annual Carnival Ball. Jack Morgan (John Wayne), dashing gambler and man-about town, has rigged the election in favor of Jenny, whom he loves. Jenny how-ever realizes that the whole affair is a farce, and this

John Wayne, Joan Blondell, and chorus

Leonid Kinskey and John Wayne

John Wayne and Joan Blondell

makes her more determined than ever to carry out her life's ambition—to break into Memphis society.

Alan Alderson (Ray Middleton), cynical and embittered scion of the decadent Alderson family, runs heavily into debt on Jenny's gambling boat. She learns that the Alderson estate is to be sold for taxes, and makes a forthright proposition to Alan. If he would marry her and give her the prestige of his name, she will clear his debts and restore the family to its former influential position. Alan accepts the bargain and marries Jenny.

Once at the Alderson estate, Jenny runs into opposition from Alan's father, Stephen Alderson (Philip Merivale) and Aunt Julia (Blanche Yurka). They are determined to make life miserable for Jenny. Jack Morgan has never stopped loving Jenny, in spite of her marriage, and he attempts to save her from humiliation whenever it is in his power to do so.

Aunt Julia becomes obsessed with her determination to rid the family of Jenny. She attempts to poison Jenny, but Alan drinks the deadly brew himself by error and dies. Jenny is brought to trial for murder. Only the testimony of Aunt Katherine (Edith Barrett), the dominated and timid sister of Aunt Julia, clears her and proves Aunt Julia the murderess. Jenny, free and happily reunited with Jack, returns with him to the gambling boat.

Running time: 87 minutes
Release date: December 29, 1941

Dewey Robinson, John Wayne, and Joan Blondell

Paulette Goddard, John Wayne, and Raymond Massey

Reap the Wild Wind

PARAMOUNT PICTURES

CAST:

Ray Milland, John Wayne, Paulette Goddard, Raymond Massey, Robert Preston, Susan Hayward, Lynne Overman, Walter Hampden, Louise Beavers, Elizabeth Risdon, Hedda Hopper, Martha O'Driscoll, Victor Kilian, Monte Blue, Charles Bickford, Janet Beecher, Barbara Britten, Mildred Harris, Victor Varconi, Julia Faye, Oscar Polk, Ben Carter, Lane Chandler, Keith Richards, Milburn Stone.

CREDITS:

Produced and directed by Cecil B. DeMille. Associate producer: William H. Pine. Associate director: Arthur Rosson. Screenplay by Alan LeMay, Charles Bennett and Jesse Lasky, Jr. Based on a *Saturday Evening Post* story by Thelma Strabel. Photographed by Victor Milner, ASC, and William V. Skall, ASC. Underwater photography by Dewey Wrigley, ASC. Special effects by Gordon Jennings, ASC, W. L. Pereira and Farciot Edouart, ASC. Edited by Anne Bauchens. Art direction by Hans Dreier and Roland Anderson. Sound recording by Harry Lindgren and John Corps. Musical score by Victor Young. Color by Technicolor.

SYNOPSIS:

Loxi Claiborne (Paulette Goddard), tomboy owner of a Key West salvage schooner, puts to sea in a hurricane with her salvage master, Capt. Philpott (Lynne Overman), to aid a ship wrecked on the Key West shoals. She finds the captain of the doomed vessel,

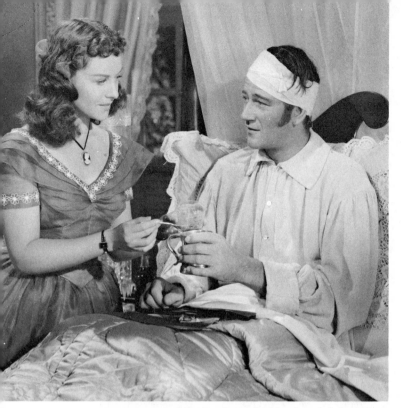

Paulette Goddard and John Wayne

Capt. Jack Stuart (John Wayne), lashed to the mast, and a rival salvage crew, head by King Cutler (Raymond Massey), already on the scene. Cutler and his brother Dan (Robert Preston) are always the first of the salvage men to reach the side of a stricken ship,

Paulette Goddard and John Wayne

as if they had some mysterious way of knowing in advance where and when a wreck would happen.

Nursed back to health by Loxi, Capt. Stuart tells her that the loss of his ship may cost him command of the Southern Cross steamship, the newest vessel of the Devereaux Line. Loxi goes to Charleston and attempts to convince Steve Tolliver (Ray Milland), sea lawyer for Devereaux, that the ship was wrecked by pirates. Tolliver, in love now with Loxi, is sent to Key West to break up the pirate ring. In his pocket is Stuart's commission as skipper of the new ship: to be given to him only when his name is cleared.

Realizing that Tolliver is dangerous, King Cutler attempts to do away with him, finally trapping him on an old sponge boat. Cutler's intention is to shanghai both Tolliver and Stuart and send them on a three-year whaling voyage. A whale of a fight follows and the pirates are beaten, but, in the battle, the Southern Cross commission falls from Tolliver's pocket. Stuart, thinking he has been double-crossed by his rival, is furious and makes a deal with Cutler to wreck the steamboat. He takes command at Havana, on the maiden run to Key West.

In a heavy fog, and with a hurricane brewing, the steamboat strikes the jagged Key West rocks and sinks.

Accused by Tolliver with wrecking the ship, Stuart is tried. A witness reveals that Drusilla Alston (Susan Hayward), Dan Cutler's sweetheart, has been on board and lost her life. To prove or disprove this story, the court adjourns to the scene of the wreck. Tolliver and Stuart, in divers' suits, descend into the murky depths and, in the green half-light of the sea, Tolliver finds Drusilla's scarf and tucks it into his belt. Suddenly the two men are attacked by a giant squid and Stuart, knowing Tolliver's testimony could send him to the gallows, saves his rival's life and loses his own. He is crushed to death by the sea monster.

When he's brought to the surface, Tolliver shows the scarf to Dan, who, mad with grief, charges his brother, King Cutler, with piracy and with causing Drusilla's death. King shoots him on the spot and is, in turn, shot to death by Tolliver.

Loxi kneels beside the dying Dan Cutler and takes his head in her arms. Her eyes meet Steve's in love and understanding.

Running time: 124 minutes
Release date: March 19, 1942

Randolph Scott, John Wayne, and Marlene Dietrich

The Spoilers

UNIVERSAL PICTURES

CAST:

John Wayne, Marlene Dietrich, Randolph Scott, Margaret Lindsay, Harry Carey, Richard Barthelmess, William Farnum, George Cleveland, Samuel S. Hinds, Marietta Canty, Robert W. Service, Russell Simpson, Jack Norton, Charles Halton, Ray Bennett.

CREDITS:

Produced by Frank Lloyd. Directed by Ray Enright. Screenplay by Lawrence Hazard and Tom Reed. Based on the novel by Rex Beach. Photographed by Milton Krasner. Art direction by Jack Otterson and John B. Goodman. Musical director: Charles Previn. Music by Frank Skinner.

SYNOPSIS:

Cherry Malottte (Marlene Dietrich) is in love with Roy Glennister (John Wayne), part owner of a gold mine. Roy, blinded by his attraction for Helen Chester (Margaret Lindsay), allows her uncle, Judge Stillman (Samuel S. Hinds) to double-cross him in a case that would decide the fate of the mine.

John Wayne and Harry Carey

When the marshal is killed, the new gold commissioner McNamara (Randolph Scott) unjustly jails Roy. Cherry opens a confession from Helen that she, Stillman and McNamara are in a conspiracy to rob the miners. Roy escapes from jail and with his partner, Destry (Harry Carey), they open the mine that has been guarded by McNamara's men. Roy returns to town, kills Stillman, and then beats McNamara in a no-holds-barred fist fight.

Running time: 84 minutes
Release date: April 13, 1942

Marlene Dietrich, John Wayne, and Randolph Scott

Marlene Dietrich and John Wayne

John Wayne and Binnie Barnes

In Old California

REPUBLIC PICTURES

CAST:

John Wayne, Binnie Barnes, Albert Dekker, Helen Parrish, Patsy Kelly, Edgar Kennedy, Dick Purcell, Harry Shannon, Charles Halton, Emmett Lynn, Bob McKenzie, Milt Kibbee, Paul Sutton, Anne O'Neal.

CREDITS:

Associate producer: Robert North. Directed by William McGann. Screenplay by Gertrude Purcell and Frances Hyland. Original story by J. Robert Bren and Gladys Atwater. Photographed by Jack Marta. Supervising editor: Murray Seldeen. Edited by Howard O'Neill. Art direction by Russell Kimball. Music by David Buttolph.

SYNOPSIS:

Tom Craig (John Wayne), a handsome, two-fisted Bostonian, travels westward to set up a business in Sacramento as a pharmacist. On his way, he meets Lacey Miller (Binnie Barnes), a glamorous dance-hall singer who is engaged to Britt Dawson (Albert Dekker), a burly overlord of Sacramento politics.

Enraged because Lacey is obviously attracted to Tom's eastern polish and charm, Britt wields his political power to forbid anyone to lease store space to him. But Lacey, captivated by Tom, agrees to become his partner in the drugstore, taking half of the profits in lieu of rent.

Britt's weak-willed younger brother Joe Dawson (Dick Purcell) has always resented the hold Lacey has on Britt, and when he learns of the business partnership, he tells Britt immediately. Britt confronts Lacey in high rage, but she deftly convinces him that the arrangement was made solely for her personal profit. Britt, to Joe's deep disgust, is content to let the matter ride.

Meanwhile, Tom endears himself to the community by curing minor aches and pains and functioning effectively in the absence of a physician. Tom remains aloof from Lacey because of her engagement to Britt, and is smitten by Ellen Sanford (Helen Parrish), a patrician visitor from San Francisco. Lacey, consumed with jealousy, tries to keep them apart. She realizes that Ellen is cold and selfish, and wants Tom only to further her own ambitious aims. But all her efforts are in vain; Tom proposes to Ellen and she accepts him.

Tom learns that the source of Britt Dawson's wealth is forced tribute from the neighboring ranchers. He incurs Dawson's further enmity by leading the ranchers in a successful revolt. Dawson is unable to avenge himself, however, because Lacey threatens to break her engagement if any harm befalls Tom.

Fuming about the situation, Britt plots Tom's downfall. He places poison in the tonic Tom prescribes to the townspeople; and when the first victim, a derelict named Whitey (Emmett Lynn) succumbs, Britt incites the townspeople to lynch Tom. The lynching is prevented in the nick of time by the news that gold has been found at Sutter's Mill. Moved by the persuasive oratory of Lacey, everyone rushes to the gold fields to stake out a claim. Depressed because his attempts to prove Britt's guilt in the poisoning are ignored, Tom prepares to leave Sacramento for San Francisco, where Ellen's father will set him up in business.

Edgar Kennedy, Harry Shannon, and John Wayne

Lacey, realizing for the first time the full extent of Britt's villainy, breaks her engagement with him and follows the gold rush. On arriving at one of the camps, she finds that a terrible epidemic has broken out, with a calamitous shortage of drugs and supplies. She sends for Tom, volunteering meanwhile to do what good she can do as a nurse until help arrives. Tom's eagerness to return and bring his skill and medical supplies to the stricken people brings about a complete break with the selfish Ellen. Britt attempts to hold up the supply wagon, planning to kill Tom and sell the badly needed supplies at fabulous prices, but Tom outwits him. Britt is mortally wounded by his own brother. Just before he dies, he absolves Tom of all blame for the poisoning.

Running time: 88 minutes
Release date: June 11, 1942

Charles Halton and John Wayne

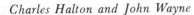

John Wayne and unidentified players

John Wayne and John Carroll

Flying Tigers

REPUBLIC PICTURES

CAST:

John Wayne, John Carroll, Anna Lee, Paul Kelly, Gordon Jones, Mae Clarke, Addison Richards, Edmund MacDonald, Bill Shirley, Tom Neal, James Dodd, Gregg Barton, John James, Chester Gan, David Bruce.

CREDITS:

Associate producer: Edmund Grainger. Directed by David Miller. Screenplay by Kenneth Gamet and Barry Trivers. Original story by Kenneth Gamet. Photographed by Jack Marta. Edited by Ernest Nims. Music by Victor Young.

SYNOPSIS:

The American Volunteer Group, or Flying Tigers, fight bravely for China's freedom despite the fact that they are greatly outnumbered by the Japs. Squadron Leader Jim Gordon (John Wayne) gets one new recruit when Woody Jason (John Carroll) joins the group.

Woody signs up only because he needs money to pay off a breach-of-promise suit. His egotism and mercenary motives gain him the ill-will of fellow fliers. He further antagonizes them by stealing Jim's girl, Brooke (Anna Lee), a Red Cross worker. He quarrels with one flier, then is blamed for the latter's death in a crash. He fails to be at the base to take one of his

124

Anna Lee and John Wayne

John Wayne and Addison Richards

regular flights and the man who takes his place is killed.

Woody begs for another chance and Jim relents. Then Woody redeems himself by saving Jim's life when the plane in which they are bombing a Japanese supply train catches fire. The wounded Woody pushes Jim out of the plane and Jim parachutes to safety. Woody at the controls, dives headlong into the train.

Running time: 101 minutes
Release date: September 23, 1942

John Wayne and Anna Lee

John Wayne, Anna Lee, and John Carroll

Moroni Olson, Joan Crawford, John Wayne, and Henry Daniell

Reunion in France

METRO-GOLDWYN-MAYER

CAST:

Joan Crawford, John Wayne, Philip Dorn, Reginald Owen, Albert Bassermann, John Carradine, Ann Ayars, Moroni Olsen, J. Edward Bromberg, Henry Daniell, Howard Da Silva, Charles Arnt, Morris Ankrum, Edith Evanson, Ernest Dorian, Margaret Laurence, Odette Myrtil, Peter Whitney, Ava Gardner.

CREDITS:

Produced by Joseph L. Mankiewicz. Directed by Jules Dassin. Screenplay by Jan Lustig. Original story by Ladislas Bus-Fekete. Photographed by Robert Planck.

SYNOPSIS:

After a brief reunion with her sweetheart Robert Cortot (Philip Dorn) whom she hears extolled on all sides for the magnificent job he has done in co-ordinating industry for the defense of France, beautiful Michele de la Becque (Joan Crawford) leaves Paris for her family's chateau on May 9, 1940. That night the Nazi hordes invade the Low Countries and then Paris falls.

Michele returns to a silent Paris, occupied by the Nazis. Her mansion has been turned into a coal allotment bureau and she is given one room in which to live. She is happy to find Robert safe but is amazed to discover that he is living gaily in his accustomed luxury. She supposes that Robert is one of the traitorous Frenchmen allowed to keep his possessions through complete cooperation with the Nazis. Michele is disillusioned and bitter. She tells Robert that she never wants to see him again.

As her income is impounded, she is forced to support herself by working as a salesgirl for Mme. Montanot (Odette Myrtil).

One night, a sick young American, Pat Talbot (John Wayne), accosts Michele on the street and asks for help. He is a wounded RAF pilot, just escaped from a prison camp. She harbors him at her house and he falls in love with her. They are almost caught, but, with Montanot's help they work out a plan for his escape. It fails and Michele is forced to call on the detested but powerful Cortot for aid. She tells him that she wants to get to America with her driver, who has lost his papers. Cortot arranges it with the military governor, but the suspicions of the Gestapo is aroused. The night that Michele and Pat are supposed

to leave for safety, Cortot himself puts them in the care of two Nazi generals. They proceed to the border. They are just about to cross when the patrol is warned by radio to watch for three important escaped English prisoners.

The party overcomes the patrol, and after an exciting chase, reaches a field in unoccupied France where Michele learns from the escaping fliers that Cortot is really a patriot, that he has helped hundreds of fliers to escape and that the war materials he sends to Germany are no good.

A British plane lands and picks up Pat and the other flyers. The next day, the military governor arrests Cortot. He has procured the passes for Michele, she is missing and had been seen with the escaping Britishers. All are astounded when Michele walks in. This clears Cortot and Michele tells him that she loves him and the great work that he is doing.

Running time: 104 minutes
Release date: December 2, 1942

John Wayne, Joan Crawford, and Philip Dorn

John Wayne, Marlene Dietrich, and Randolph Scott

Pittsburgh

UNIVERSAL PICTURES

CAST:

Marlene Dietrich, John Wayne, Randolph Scott, Frank Craven, Louise Allbritton, Thomas Gomez, Ludwig Stossel, Shemp Howard, Sammy Stein, Paul Fix, John Dilson, Samuel S. Hinds, Douglas Fowley, Virginia Sale, Bess Flowers, Mira McKinney.

CREDITS:

Produced by Charles K. Feldman. Directed by Lewis Seiler. Original story by George Olsen and Tom Reed. Screenplay by Kenneth Gamet and Tom Reed. Photographed by Robert DeGrasse. Music by Frank Skinner.

SYNOPSIS:

Pittsburgh "Pitt" Markham (John Wayne) and his miner pal Cash Evans (Randolph Scott) meet Josie Winters (Marlene Dietrich). Using a forged contract, Pitt turns a coal mine "on paper" into a huge corporation. Forgetting Josie, Pitt marries Shannon Prentiss (Louise Allbritton), daughter of a steel magnate.

Pitt's drive for power separates him from Cash and his friends. Shannon leaves Pitt, and he learns Josie has married Cash. Then comes Pearl Harbor and Pitt's firm is swamped with war orders. Pitt, a changed man, resumes his partnership with Cash. The two men, working with scientist Doc Powers (Frank Craven) not only set production records which earn a citation of merit from the government, but also make a magnificent contribution to the war effort with the discovery of a revolutionary coal-tar formula.

Running time: 98 minutes
Release date December 7, 1942

Randolph Scott and John Wayne

Jean Arthur and John Wayne

Lady Takes a Chance

("The Cowboy and the Girl")

RKO RADIO PICTURES

CAST:

Jean Arthur, John Wayne, Charles Winninger, Phil Silvers, Mary Field, Don Costello, John Philliber, Grady Sutton, Grant Withers, Hans Conreid, Peggy Carroll, Ariel Heath, Sugar Geise, Joan Blair.

CREDITS:

Produced by Frank Ross. Associate producer: Richard Ross. Directed by William A. Seiter. Screenplay by Robert Ardrey. Original story by Jo Swerling. Photographed by Frank Redman, ASC. Edited by Theron Warth. Music by Roy Webb. Art direction by Albert S. D'Agostino. Assistant director: J. D. Starkey.

SYNOPSIS:

Mollie Truesdale (Jean Arthur), a New York bank clerk, has saved her pennies for a bus tour of the West. Three jealous guys are at the bus station to see her off. The days aren't breathless and there are no fellas. That is, until the bus stops in Fairfield, Oregon, and Mollie goes to the rodeo and meets Duke Hudkins (John Wayne). He was bucked off his horse right into her lap. Now Mollie knows why she came West.

That evening she has the greatest time of her life with Duke, shooting craps, drinking and getting into a fight. Mollie misses her bus. When she can't get a room, Duke offers to let her use his. He even makes his sidekick Waco (Charles Winninger), sleep

on the porch while Duke sleeps on the pool table. Mollie is forced to travel with Duke and Waco in order to meet her bus. When they are camping on the desert, Mollie takes the blanket from Duke's horse, Sammy. In the morning Sammy is sick. When Mollie sees Duke's concern over his horse she wishes Duke could love her as much. She goes to work on Duke at a trailer camp. Mollie cooked dinner and Duke was wiping the dishes when he realized he had an apron around his waist. He walks out.

The bus trip back is a dreary affair for Mollie. She is met by the same three boy friends. But Duke looms up big and protective, distributes the boy friends around the waiting room and plants her firmly back in the bus. Mollie again is off for the West. But this time it will be different.

Running time: 86 minutes
Release date: August 19, 1943

John Wayne and Jean Arthur

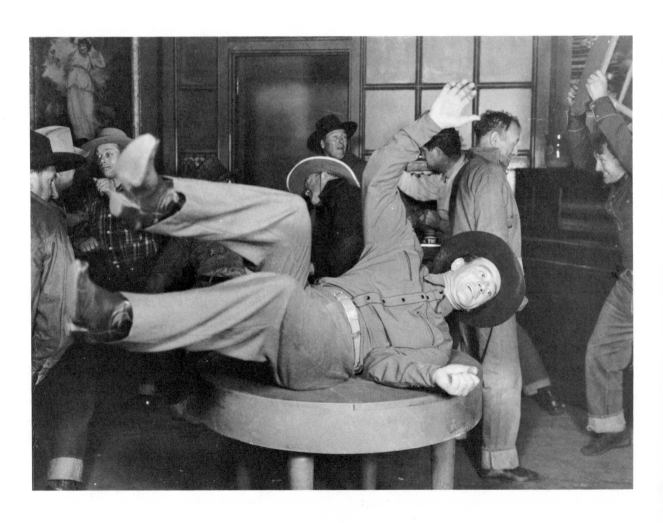

Albert Dekker, John Wayne, and Martha Scott

War of the Wildcats

(Formerly titled "In Old Oklahoma")

REPUBLIC PICTURES

CAST:

John Wayne, Martha Scott, Albert Dekker, George "Gabby" Hayes, Marjorie Rambeau, Dale Evans, Grant Withers, Sidney Blackmer, Paul Fix, Cecil Cunningham, Irving Bacon, Anne O'Neal.

CREDITS:

Associate producer: Robert North. Directed by Albert S. Rogell. Original story and adaptation by Thomson Burtis. Screenplay by Ethel Hill and Eleanore Griffith. Photographed by Jack Marta. Edited by Ernest Nims. Art direction by Russell Kimball. Musical score by Walter Scharf.

SYNOPSIS:

Cathy Allen (Martha Scott), attractive and independent, having written a very daring book, is obliged to leave the small town where she has been teaching school. She goes to Sapulpa, Oklahoma, where she meets Jim Gardner (Albert Dekker), a prosperous oil operator, and Dan Somers (John Wayne), attractive cowboy. Because of their mutual interest in Cathy, there is antagonism between the two men.

Bessie Baxter (Marjorie Rambeau) who runs the hotel takes Cathy under her wing. Jim tries to lease Indian land, rich in oil, but Dan advises the Indians against accepting the offer. Wards of the government, the Indians urge Dan to take over the oil lease.

John Wayne and Martha Scott

Washington gives its approval with the provision that he make delivery to the refinery at Tulsa by a specified date.

Lack of equipment, obstacles placed in his way by Jim who is now Dan's bitter enemy, and a misunderstanding with Cathy, all go towards discouraging Dan. The deadline day arrives—Dan and his men are ready. They have doggedly worked day and night, and now they rush the oil to Tulsa with only minutes to spare.

Cathy and Dan make up their misunderstanding, and Jim, realizing he has lost Cathy and also his big land grab scheme, decides to work with Dan instead of against him.

Running time: 102 minutes
Release date: October 25, 1943

George "Gabby" Hayes and John Wayne

John Wayne and Albert Dekker

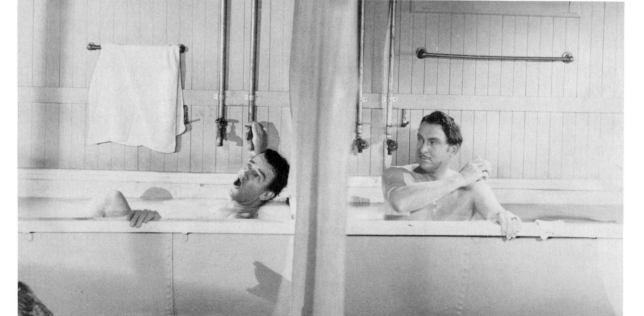

Dennis O'Keefe, John Wayne, and unidentified players

The Fighting Seabees

REPUBLIC PICTURES

CAST:

John Wayne, Susan Hayward, Dennis O'Keefe, William Frawley, Addison Richards, Leonid Kinskey, Paul Fix, J. M. Kerrigan, Ben Welden, Grant Withers, Duncan Renaldo.

CREDITS:

Associate producer: Albert J. Cohen. Directed by Howard Lydecker and Edward Ludwig. Screenplay by Borden Chase and Aeneas MacKenzie. Original story by Borden Chase. Photographed by William Bradford. Edited by Richard Van Enger. Musical score by Walter Scharf.

SYNOPSIS:

Early in the war, many civilian workers in the Pacific area were killed by Japs because they were prohibited by law to be armed. Construction chief Wedge Donovon (John Wayne) and Lt. Comdr. Bob Yarrow (Dennis O'Keefe) join forces in Washington to create a new branch of service. Through their efforts, construction battalions of men, equipped to fight as well as build, are attached to the Navy.

Wedge becomes an officer in the newly formed Seabees. Assigned to the island of which Bob is commander, Bob tells the hot-headed Wedge that all snipers must be ignored, that building is his main job now. Wedge obeys orders until his pal is killed, and then he orders his men to clear out the Japs. During a fog, more Japs land to surround the Americans and threaten a valuable oil depot. The wounded Bob tells Wedge that the oil must be saved at all cost.

Aware that his own stubbornness has brought about the situation, Wedge rights it the only way he can. He rushes into the thick of battle and ignites one oil tank which completely wipes out the Japs. The action costs Wedge his life, but the Americans and the tanks of oil are saved.

Running time: 100 minutes
Release date: January 19, 1944

John Wayne and Ella Raines

Tall in the Saddle

RKO RADIO PICTURES

CAST:

John Wayne, Ella Raines, Ward Bond, George "Gabby" Hayes, Audrey Long, Elisabeth Risdon, Don Douglas, Paul Fix, Russell Wade, Emory Parnell, Raymond Hatton, Harry Woods, Wheaton Chambers, Frank Puglia, Bob McKenzie.

CREDITS:

Produced by Robert Fellows. Directed by Edwin L. Marin. Screenplay by Michael Hogan and Paul J. Fix. Original story by Gordon Ray Young. Associate producer: Theron Warth. Photographed by Robert de Grasse, ASC. Special effects by Vernon L. Walker, ASC. Edited by Philip Martin, Jr. Art direction by Albert D'Agostino and Ralph Berger. Music by Roy Webb. Musical director: C. Bakaleinikoff. Assistant director: Harry Scott.

SYNOPSIS:

Arriving in Santa Inez to take over as foreman of the KC Ranch, tall, taciturn Rocklin (John Wayne) learns that the man who had hired him, Red Cardell, has been murdered. He meets Clara (Audrey Long), heiress of the murdered man; her aunt, Miss Martin (Elisabeth Risdon), and the stage driver, Dave (Gabby Hayes). Since the girl and her aunt are in charge of the ranch, Rocklin refuses the job because he dislikes working for women. He has a prompt run-in with Clint Harolday (Russell Wade), hot-headed young gambler, and with Clews (Paul Fix), the sheriff's furtive assistant, causing trouble with Arly (Ella Raines), Clint's half-sister, a lovely spitfire who subsequently insists that her stepfather, Harolday (Don Douglas), who administers her Santee Ranch, hire Rocklin so she can have the pleasure of firing him. Actually Arly is fascinated by Rocklin, is furiously jealous of Clara. Rocklin receives a letter from Clara asking his help because her aunt is turning her affairs over to the doubtful Judge Garvey (Ward Bond). She wants to recover a letter which proves her to be of age and privileged to handle her own affairs.

In searching for the letter during Garvey's absence, Rocklin finds marked cards. He confronts the man with his discovery, and in a knock-down drag-out brawl leaves Garvey unconscious. Rocklin then has Clint come to his room for questioning. A hand reaches through the window, takes Rocklin's gun from his holster, shoots and kills Clint, tosses the gun back in the room, disappears. Found with the body of a man shot with his gun, things look bad for Rocklin who refuses to surrender to the sheriff, and makes his getaway pursued by a posse. He gets to the KC Ranch where he overhears Miss Martin telling Clara that Rocklin is the lawful owner of the ranch because he was the nephew of Cardell, the murdered owner.

John Wayne and George "Gabby" Hayes

That's why she and Garvey destroyed the missing letter, which incidentally revealed these facts.

Arly arrives, reveals that Harolday killed both Cardell and Clint; the former because he wanted his land, the latter because he knew too much, and that Garvey was working for Harolday to capture the KC from Clara. Even Miss Martin was in on part of the plot. Harolday is killed by Juan, Arly's devoted bodyguard. Rocklin, despite evidences of her temper, decides that Arly would make a perfect Mrs. Rocklin and Arly had thought so, too.

Running time: 87 minutes
Release date: September 29, 1944

John Wayne and Ella Raines

John Wayne, William Frawley, Ann Dvorak, and Joseph Schildkraut

Flame of the Barbary Coast

REPUBLIC PICTURES

CAST:

John Wayne, Ann Dvorak, Joseph Schildkraut, William Frawley, Virginia Grey, Russell Hicks, Jack Norton, Paul Fix, Manart Kippen, Eve Lynne, Marc Lawrence, Butterfly McQueen, Rex Lease, Hank Bell, Al Murphy.

CREDITS:

Associate producer-director: Joseph Kane. Screenplay by Borden Chase. Photographed by Robert de Grasse, ASC. Edited by Richard L. Van Enger. Art direction by Gano Chittenden. Special effects by Howard and Theodore Lydecker. Musical director: Morton Scott. Sound by Earl Crain, Sr.

SYNOPSIS:

Duke Fergus (John Wayne), strapping Montana cattleman, visits San Francisco to collect $500 owed him by Tito Morell (Joseph Schildkraut). Morell, aristocratic blacksheep owner of El Dorado, a roaring gambling joint, is the smooth, undisputed boss of the Barbary Coast who believes suckers are born to be taken.

Arriving at the El Dorado, Duke meets Flaxen Tarry (Ann Dvorak), a beautiful creature who has earned the name of the Flame of Barbary Coast. She and Tito are engaged. Duke decides to play his $500 at the El Dorado, and Flaxen offers to serve as his guide to pique Tito, who has been too attentive to Rita Dane (Virginia Grey), a blonde singer. Under

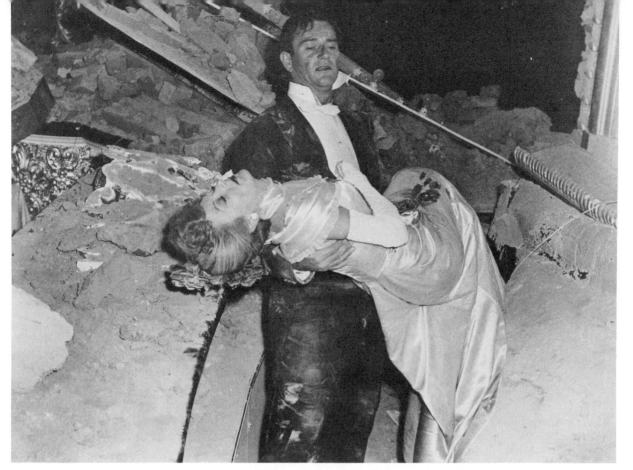

John Wayne and Ann Dvorak

John Wayne, Ann Dvorak, and unidentified players

Ann Dvorak and John Wayne

another bankroll which he has made through a cattle sale. This time Duke is more of a match for Tito for he is accompanied by Smooth Wylie (William Frawley), a professional gambler. Duke cleans Tito of most of his money, and also takes care of such Coast characters as Horseshoe Brown (Al Murphy) and Calico Jim (Paul Fix).

Calico yelps for the assistance of his pal, tough Jot Disko (Marc Lawrence), but Tito insists that to kill the rancher would only provoke Cyrus Danver (Russell Hicks), newspaper publisher, and others who are waiting for the opportunity to clean up the Barbary Coast. But Disko provokes a gun fight with Duke. Duke wings him and decides to remain in San Francisco to win Flaxen. He invests his money in the construction of The Silver Dollar, a competitive gambling place opposite Tito's, and gets Flaxen to star in his show.

On opening night, Flaxen makes her gala appearance on the stage. While she is singing, the earthquake hits. The chandeliers start to sway, pillars begin crumbling, and the patrons become panic-stricken as all San Francisco is thrown into confusion. Flaxen is hurt badly—paralyzed for a time. But as San Francisco recovers, so does she. And all is well that ends well.

Flaxen's expert guidance, Duke wins heavily. After Flaxen leaves, Tito, by crooked means, cleans Duke out of every cent he had. Flaxen gives him a railroad ticket back to Montana. Duke asks her to go with him, but Flaxen is reluctant to quit the Coast, and he leaves without her.

Duke is not one to be beaten so easily, however, and before long he returns to San Francisco—with

Running time: 91 minutes
Release date: April 18, 1945

Joseph Schildkraut, John Wayne, William Frawley, Paul Fix, and Marc Lawrence

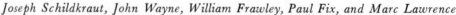

Back to Bataan

RKO RADIO PICTURES

CAST:

John Wayne, Anthony Quinn, Beulah Bondi, Fely Franquelli, Leonard Strong, Richard Loo, Philip Ahn, "Ducky" Louie, Lawrence Tierney, Paul Fix, Abner Biberman, Vladimir Sokoloff, J. Alex Havier.

CREDITS:

Produced by Robert Fellows. Associate producer: Theron Warth. Directed by Edward Dmytryk. Screenplay by Ben Barzman and Richard Landau. Original story by Aeneas MacKenzie and William Gordon. Photographed by Nicholas Musuraca, ASC. Music by Roy Webb. Musical director: C. Bakaleinikoff. Art direction by Albert S. D'Agostino and Ralph Berger. Edited by Marston Fay. Assistant director: Ruby Rosenberg.

SYNOPSIS:

On Bataan, Colonel Joseph Madden (John Wayne) listens, as the officers and men on Corregidor listen to the radio voice of Dalisay Delgado (Fely Franquelli), one-time popular Filipino movie star, pleading with her countrymen to cease resisting the Japs. It is apparent to all that their plight is hopeless, that they cannot expect reinforcements or badly needed supplies. With Madden is Captain Andres Bonifacio (Anthony Quinn), of the Philippine Scouts, who loved

141

Dalisay and is heartbroken because she has turned traitor.

With the fall of Bataan inevitable, Madden is ordered out to organize guerrilla resistance among U.S. and Filipino troops who have been cut off and fugitive Filipino citizens. The Japs arrive and hang the school's principal because he refuses to lower the American flag. Bertha Barnes (Beulah Bondi), American teacher, escapes and joins Madden's forces. With her is the boy Maximo (Ducky Louie), one of her pupils. One of the first acts the guerrillas perform is to hang the Jap officer responsible for the principal's death.

Madden plans to get the aid of the Katipunan, a secret society powerful in Filipino revolutionary days, through Bonifacio who is a grandson of the original leader, whom he rescues from the infamous March of Death of the prisoners from Bataan. Meanwhile General MacArthur goes to Australia, and Corregidor surrenders. Bonifacio, embittered because American aid has not been forthcoming, refuses to further sacrifice his countrymen by calling out the Katipunan. He consents, however, to take a message to Manila. There he is delighted to learn his contact is Dalisay. She tells him she has sacrificed herself to the Jap Colonel Kuroki (Philip Ahn) to learn vital military information which she has conveyed to MacArthur in her seemingly treasonable broadcasts. Bonifacio decides to call out the Katipunan and stay in the fight.

Alarmed over the growing power of the guerrillas, the Japs decide to give the Filipinos their "independence" in a ceremony to be held at Balintowak. But in a daring coup Madden's men annihilate the Japs during the ceremony.

The Japs capture the boy Maximo and torture him until he consents to lead them to the guerrilla headquarters. But Maximo steers the truck in which he, Jap officers and a detachment of soldiers are riding, over a steep cliff, and all perish. Two years pass and with the approach of General MacArthur and the landing on Leyte, the guerrillas cut the ground from under the Japanese defenses and aid American Rangers deliver the prisoners of the enemy at Cabanatuan.

Running time: 97 minutes
Release date: May 31, 1945

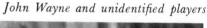

John Wayne and unidentified players

Mike Mazurki, John Wayne, Grant Withers, Paul Fix, Vera Hruba Ralston, and Jack LaRue

Dakota

REPUBLIC PICTURES

CAST:

John Wayne, Vera Hruba Ralston, Walter Brennan, Ward Bond, Ona Munson, Hugo Haas, Mike Mazurki, Olive Blakeney, Paul Fix, Nicodemus Stewart, Grant Withers, Robert Livingston, George Cleveland, Jack LaRue, Bobby Blake, Robert Barret, Sarah Padden, Claire DuBrey, Ward Bond.

CREDITS:

Associate producer: Joseph Kane. Directed by Joseph Kane. Screenplay by Lawrence Hazard. Adaptation by Howard Estabrook. Original story by Carl Foreman. Photographed by Jack Marta. Edited by Fred Allen. Art direction by Russell Kimball and Gano Chittenden. Second unit director: Yakima Canutt. Sound by Fred Stahl. Musical score by Walter Scharf. Song "Coax Me" by Andrew Sterling and Harry Von Tilzer.

SYNOPSIS:

John Devlin (John Wayne) elopes with the daughter of railroad tycoon Marko Poli (Hugo Haas). Sandy (Vera Hruba Ralston), the new bride, decides that they should settle down in North Dakota, instead of California. Sandy heard her father say that the railroad will be extended to Dakota—and she plans to buy options on land and sell to the railroad at a profit. Devlin relents—but finally agrees with her.

143

Vera Hruba Ralston, John Wayne, Ward Bond, and Mike Mazurki

John Wayne and Vera Hruba Ralston

On the stagecoach to Ft. Abercrombie, Devlin and Sandy meet Jim Bender (Ward Bond) and Bigtree Collins (Mike Mazurki). These two men practically own the town of Fargo. They find out the purpose of Devlin's trip and plan to protect their little empire. They already are trying to drive out the bonanza farmers—burning their property, destroying their wheat, blaming this devastation on the Indians.

Aboard the River Bird, Devlin and Sandy meet Capt. Bounce (Walter Brennan) a picturesque old seafarer. During the trip, two of Bender's henchmen—Slagin (Grant Withers) and Carp (Paul Fix), board the River Bird and at gunpoint relieve Devlin of his money belt. They escape from a chase, when Capt. Bounce unexpectedly lands on a sandbar and sinks the River Bird.

At Fargo, the land war begins. Devlin teams up with the wheat farmers against Bender and his gang. Several unsuccessful attempts on Devlin's life are made by the gang. Finally, at Bender's request, Devlin agrees to leave town, if his money is returned to him. Bender consents, and then has the hotel surrounded by his gang. Devlin slugs it out with Slagin and Carp, and then goes looking for Bender. Collins kills Bender in a fight over the Devlin loot. Overtaking Collins, Devlin defeats him in a fight-to-the-finish and recovers his money. The Cavalry from the Fort arrives on the scene—and soon restores order in the town.

Running time: 82 minutes
Release date: November 2, 1945

Walter Brennan, John Wayne, and Vera Hruba Ralston

John Wayne, Donna Reed, and Robert Montgomery

They Were Expendable

METRO-GOLDWYN-MAYER

CAST:

Robert Montgomery, John Wayne, Donna Reed, Jack Holt, Ward Bond, Marshall Thompson, Paul Langton, Leon Ames, Arthur Walsh, Donald Curtis, Cameron Mitchell, Jeff York, Murray Alper, Harry Tenbrook, Jack Pennick, Alex Havier, Charles Trowbridge, Robert Barrat, Bruce Kellog, Tim Murdock, Louis Jean Heydt, Russell Simpson, Vernon Steele.

CREDITS:

Produced by John Ford. Directed by John Ford. Screenplay by Lt. Commander Frank Wead. Original story by William L. White. Photographed by Joseph H. August. Music by Herbert Stothart. Sound by Douglas Shearer. Edited by Frank E. Hull and Douglas Biggs. Art direction by Cedric Gibbons and Malcolm Brown.

SYNOPSIS:

Until Pearl Harbor the squadron of P-T boats at Manila Bay were regarded by complacent officers as little more than pleasure craft. War suddenly gives the P-T boats a new and important significance, thanks to the efforts of two of their skippers, Lt. John Brickley (Robert Montgomery) and Lt. (j.g.) Rusty Ryan (John Wayne).

This pair, and their crews, have long believed that the tiny, high-powered craft, equipped with guns and torpedo tubes, could slip into Jap infested harbors under cover of darkness, loose their torpedoes, and return with a maximum of safety. They are given an opportunity to prove this theory when the Philippines are blockaded after the Pearl Harbor attack.

First objective is a Jap cruiser in Subic Bay. Two P-T boats glide through mine-filled waters and sink the cruiser, but only at the cost of one P-T boat and some of the men. From then on, the P-T boats are allowed to go on regular nightly raids.

In the meantime, Ryan has been in sick bay, where he meets and falls in love with a pretty Army nurse named Sandy Davyss (Donna Reed). Their romance is interrupted when the P-T boats are given their most important assignment so far—to evacuate a General (Robert Barrat) and his family, Admiral Blackwell (Charles Trowbridge) and a few other high-ranking officers from beleaguered Bataan. The hazardous trip will mean that both boats and crews are "expendable"—any straggler which runs into difficulty will get no help from the others. The important cargo is delivered to its destination, Mindanao, at the cost of two of Brickley's four remaining boats.

Robert Montgomery and John Wayne

Ward Bond, Robert Montgomery, and John Wayne

Robert Montgomery, Donald Curtis,
John Wayne, and Bruce Kellog

The admiral turns Brickley and his men over to the Mindanao Army commander, General Martin (Jack Holt), who will make use of the boats to knock out Jap supply ships. Then comes an assignment to knock out a big Jap cruiser. The desperate encounter is successful but on the return trip Brickley has to beach his crippled P-T boat and Ryan loses his when it is machinegunned by a Jap plane.

The two crews are separated. Ryan sends his few remaining men off to join Army forces and he starts through the jungle alone, in an effort to find Brickley. He finds him as he is turning his crippled boat over to the Army. They are about to join fleeing Army troops themselves when General Martin catches up to them with new orders. They and two of their men are to be flown back to Australia, thence to the United States.

Running time: 136 minutes
Release date: November 23, 1945

Robert Montgomery, Donna Reed, and John Wayne

Anne Triola, John Wayne, Claudette Colbert, and Don DeFore

Without Reservations

RKO RADIO PICTURES

CAST:

John Wayne, Claudette Colbert, Don DeFore, Anne Triola, Phil Brown, Frank Puglia, Dona Drake, Thurston Hall, Fernando Alvarado, Charles Arnt, Louella Parsons.

CREDITS:

Produced by Jesse L. Lasky. Directed by Mervyn Le-Roy. Screenplay by Andrew Solt. From the novel by Jane Allen and Mae Livingston. Photographed by Milton Krasner, ASC. Special effects by Vernon L. Walker, ASC, Russell A. Cully, ASC, Clifford Stine. Edited by Jack Ruggiero and Harold Stine. Art direction by Albert S. D'Agostino and Ralph Berger. Production assistant: William H. Cannon. Music by Roy Webb. Musical director: C. Bakaleinikoff. Assistant director: Lloyd Richards. Sound by Clem Portman and Francis M. Sarver.

SYNOPSIS:

Kit Madden (Claudette Colbert), author of a best-selling novel, is on her way to Hollywood to work on the screen version. She has an upper berth to Chicago. In the lower is Capt. Rusty (John Wayne), a Marine flyer, and across the aisle is his pal, Lt. Dink Watson (Don DeFore). Acquaintanceship ripens fast when Kit's novel is discussed, and the two boys give it a good panning, not knowing her identity. Rusty interests Kit. She sees in him the ideal hero for her picture, and wires her producer to that effect.

At Chicago she has a drawing room reserved, but finds that the boys have reservations on another train. She can't lose sight of Rusty now. Besides, she is beginning to fall in love with him. So, minus baggage, reservation or ticket, she boards their train. That night in the club car, Kit and her two companions get a little high, and Rusty and Dink attempt to teach Kit to fly. They build a plane out of the furni-

John Wayne and Claudette Colbert

ture with very disastrous results, and Kit is thrown off the train. Her two Marines join her, and they buy a second-hand car and continue their trek. One night when Dink is repairing their car, Kit and Rusty sit in the haystack and confess their love.. Kit is worried because she has deceived Rusty over the authorship of the novel and has given him a false name.

In New Mexico, Kit cashes a check with her real name. The townspeople are about to lionize her, when a premature news story announces her arrival in Hollywood and she is thrown into jail on a bad check charge. The boys sell the car to bail her out, and as they are about to rescue her, her producer turns up and fixes things. Kit's secret is out, and Rusty goes to sulk at the Marine Base in San Diego, believing she has played him for a sucker.

Kit plunges into the Hollywood whirl. An actor is found to star in her picture. Louella Parsons, in a radio broadcast, hints at a romance between him and Kit, which doesn't please Rusty a bit. Dink keeps up a correspondence with Kit and does his best in the role of Cupid. Finally his efforts succeed, and Rusty wires he is coming to Hollywood. As Kit sees him approaching her door she lifts her head to heaven and says fervently, *Thanks, God, I'll take it from here,* the aviator's prayer of thanks for getting out of a tight spot.

Running time: 107 minutes
Release date: May 13, 1946

Don DeFore and John Wayne

John Wayne, Harry Carey, and Gail Russell

Angel and the Badman

REPUBLIC PICTURES

CAST:

John Wayne, Gail Russell, Harry Carey, Bruce Cabot, Irene Rich, Lee Dixon, Tom Powers, John Halloran, Stephen Grant, Joan Barton, Paul Hurst, Craig Woods, Marshall Reed.

CREDITS:

Produced by John Wayne. Written and directed by James Edward Grant. Photographed by A. J. Stout, ASC. Edited by Harry Keller. Production designed by Ernest Fegté. Second unit direction by Yakima Canutt. Musical score by Richard Hageman. Musical director: Cy Fever. Songs by Kim Gannon and Walter Kent.

SYNOPSIS:

Pursued by a group of armed horsemen, Quirt Evans (John Wayne), injured and desperately tired, is taken in by Quaker Thomas Worth (John Halloran), his daughter (Irene Rich) and granddaughter Prudence (Gail Russell). They ignore the warning of Dr. Mangrum (Tom Powers) to get rid of Quirt if they want to keep the peace.

During his convalescence, Quirt is attracted by Prudence, but feels he must fulfill his vow to kill Laredo Stevens (Bruce Cabot), murderer of his foster-father. While the Worths are at a Friends meeting, Quirt and his two buddies hold up a gambling train owned by Stevens. When the job is over, Quirt, to the

151

John Wayne and Gail Russell

amazement of his friends, rides back to the Worth ranch.

Quirt's love for Prudence is so strong that he promises to spare Laredo and give up his gun if she will marry him and settle down on a farm. The pledge is forgotten, however, when the couple is attacked by Stevens and his men, who chase them into a river and leaves them to drown. But Quirt manages to rescue the girl, who becomes dangerously ill. He takes his gun and rides into town in search of Stevens.

Prudence follows and finds Quirt waiting for Stevens in front of the town saloon. He silently hands her his gun, unaware that Stevens is standing down the street; gun trained on him. Stevens is about to pull the trigger when he falls to the ground, shot by Marshal Wistful McClintock (Harry Carey).

Running time: 100 minutes
Release date: February 15, 1947

Harry Carey, John Wayne, and Gail Russell

Anthony Quinn, John Wayne, and Harry Woods

Tycoon

RKO RADIO PICTURES

CAST:

John Wayne, Laraine Day, Sir Cedric Hardwicke, Judith Anderson, James Gleason, Anthony Quinn, Grant Withers, Paul Fix, Fernando Alvarado, Harry Woods, Michael Harvey, Charles Trowbridge.

CREDITS:

Produced by Stephen Ames. Directed by Richard Wallace. Screenplay by Borden Chase and John Twist. Adapted from the novel by C. E. Scoggins. Photographed by Harry J. Wild, ASC and W. Howard Greene, ASC. Technicolor color director: Natalie Kalmus. Edited by Frank Doyle. Art direction by Albert S. D'Agostino and Carroll Clark. Music by Leigh Harline. Musical direction by C. Bakaleinikoff. Special effects by Vernon L. Walker, ASC. Sound by John L. Cass and Clem Portman. Assistant director: Grayson Rogers. Color by Technicolor.

SYNOPSIS:

Frederick Alexander (Sir Cedric Hardwicke), an American industrial tycoon, contracts with Johnny Munroe (John Wayne) and his partner, Mathews (James Gleason), to build a railroad from his mines in the Andes to the coast. Johnny wants to bridge a river, but Alexander insists on a shorter line involving a tunnel. The tunneled rock proves treacherous. Conflict arises between the engineer and the magnate, who is furthr resentful when the younger man is attracted to his lovely half-Spanish daughter, Maura (Laraine Day). Maura continues to meet Munroe secretly, with the tacit approval of her duenna (Judith Anderson) and of her handsome cousin Enrique (Anthony Quinn).

Alexander grimly decides to break the upstart engineer by holding up supplies, and he also secludes Maura. Munroe and his crew keep at the tunnel despite the danger. Maura slips away for a rendezvous with Munroe. The two get lost in the jungle and have to spend the night at an old Inca ruin. Whereupon Alexander decrees an immediate marriage to satisfy his ideas of honor. Maura goes to live with Munroe at the construction camp, but is unhappy. Presently half the tunnel caves in, killing one worker. Maura, feeling disillusioned, returns to her father.

Munroe deliberately dynamites the tunnel, and proceeds to build the bridge. Mathews and most of the foremen quit, but Munroe drives on, after his arrogance alienates his top crew. With reluctant admiration Alexander offers the engineer a ninety-day extension, but the offer is spurned. When only one span remains to be put in, Munroe meets Maura and tells her that some day he'll come back and claim her.

John Wayne and Sir Cedric Hardwicke

Laraine Day, John Wayne, and Anthony Quinn

A mountain storm imperils the bridge site, but without his foreman Munroe is helpless. Single-handed he toils to save the structure. He has given up, when Maura arrives with the old crew, and by Herculean efforts most of the bridge is saved. With Alexander's blessing, Munroe and Maura are reunited to go on and complete the job—together. Alexander, meanwhile, has found romance on his own with Maura's duenna, and leaves on a honeymoon.

Running time: 126 minutes
Release date: December 3, 1947

Paul Fix, John Wayne,
unidentified player, and Michael Harvey

Henry Fonda, George O'Brien, and John Wayne

Fort Apache

An Argosy Pictures Production

RKO RADIO PICTURES

CAST:

John Wayne, Henry Fonda, Shirley Temple, Pedro Armendariz, Ward Bond, Irene Rich, John Agar, George O'Brien, Anna Lee, Victor McLaglen, Dick Foran, Jack Pennick, Guy Kibbee, Grant Withers, Mae Marsh, Miguel Inclan, Movita, Mary Gordon, Francis Ford, Frank Ferguson.

CREDITS:

Produced by John Ford and Merian C. Cooper. Directed by John Ford. Screenplay by Frank S. Nugent. Suggested by the *Saturday Evening Post* story "Mas-

sacre," by James Warner Bellah. Photographed by A. J. Stout, ASC. Edited by Jack Murray. Art direction by James Basevi. Musical score by Richard Hageman. Production manager: Bernard McEveety. Assistant director: Lowell Farrell. Sound by Frank Websted and Sam Donner.

SYNOPSIS:

Lt. Col. Thursday (Henry Fonda) is sent from the East to take command of Fort Apache in the Arizona desert. Bitter because he has been demoted from his Civil War rank of general, he thinks only of winning fame and glory so he can return to army importance.

At the Fort, the hard-bitten veterans of Apache campaigning resent the colonel's obvious scorn of them and his utter ignorance of Indian fighting. They include Captain York (John Wayne), Captain Collingwood (George O'Brien), young Lt. O'Rourke (John Agar), son of Sergeant-Major O'Rourke (Ward Bond), and sergeants Beaufort, Mulcahy and Quincannon (Pedro Armendariz, Victor McLaglen and Dick Foran).

Romance quickly springs up between the colonel's daughter (Shirley Temple) and Lt. O'Rourke, but the colonel frowns at the idea of his child marrying a noncom's son, and his insistence on rigid discipline arouses the antagonism of his men.

Finally the colonel's burning ambition sees its opportunity. Cochise (Miguel Inclan), chief of the Apaches, resenting the corrupt tactics of the local agent, leads his tribe across the border into Mexico, thereby attracting national attention. If he can bring them back, the colonel feels his reputation will be made.

He sends Captain York and Sergeant Beaufort to arrange a meeting. Cochise, trusting York's word, brings his people back over the line. But the colonel, instead of arriving with a small bodyguard as he has promised, appears with his entire command and arrogantly orders Cochise to start back to the reservation or take the consequences.

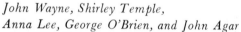

John Wayne, Shirley Temple,
Anna Lee, George O'Brien, and John Agar

Captain York protests this rash step, but the colonel accuses him of cowardice, and attacks. But Cochise, a brilliant strategist, throws his thousand warriors at the smaller cavalry force and wipes it out, save for Captain York's little detail guarding a commissary cache.

And back at Fort Apache Captain York, for the good of the service and the memory of his fallen comrades, covers up the colonel's blunder to allow his name to live on in the army's annals of heroism.

Running time: 128 minutes
Release date: March 9, 1948

[*REVIEW*]

"A rootin', tootin', Wild West show, full of Indians and the United States cavalry. . . . John Wayne is powerful, forthright and exquisitely brave."
        Bosley Crowther, *The New York Times*

"*Fort Apache* is a visually absorbing celebration of violent deeds. John Wayne is excellent as a captain who escapes the slaughter and protects his superior's name for the sake of the service."
        Howard Barnes, *New York Herald Tribune*

John Wayne, Grant Withers, and Henry Fonda

John Wayne and Montgomery Clift

Red River

Monterey Productions

UNITED ARTISTS

CAST:

John Wayne, Montgomery Clift, Walter Brennan, Joanne Dru, Harry Carey, Sr., John Ireland, Coleen Gray, Harry Carey, Jr., Noah Berry, Jr., Paul Fix, Tom Tyler, Lane Chandler, Shelley Winters.

CREDITS:

Produced and directed by Howard Hawks. Executive producer: Charles K. Feldman. Screenplay by Borden Chase and Charles Schnee. From the *Saturday Evening Post* story "The Chisholm Trail" by Borden Chase. Music composed and directed by Dimitri Tiomkin. Photographed by Russell Harlan, ASC. Edited by Christian Nyby. Art direction by John Datu Arensma.

SYNOPSIS:

The end of the Civil War finds Thomas Dunson (John Wayne) master of a vast cattle domain in Texas, but because the South is so impoverished there is no market for his herd. He decides to head, with his foster-son, Matthew Garth (Montgomery Clift), the first cattle drive over the now-famous Chisholm Trail, past the Red River, into Missouri. The way is filled with hardship for both man and beast, and eventually Dunson and Garth quarrel bitterly, with Garth deserting Dunson, who has lost control of the drive. Garth changes the direction from Missouri to Abilene, Kansas, where the new railroad will open up a huge market with the East.

Here the infuriated Dunson catches up with his foster-son and they fight it out with bare fists until

John Wayne and Montgomery Clift

John Wayne and Walter Brennan

Tess Millay (Joanne Dru) with whom Garth is in love, patches things up between them. Dunson starts things right now by making Garth a full partner in the Dunson ranch.

Running time: 125 minutes
Release date: July 14, 1948

[*REVIEW*]

"He [Howard Hawks] has got several fine performances out of a solidly masculine cast, topped off by a withering job of acting a boss-wrangler done by Mr. Wayne. This consistently able portrayer of two-fisted, two-gunned outdoor men surpasses himself in this picture."

Bosley Crowther, *The New York Times*

"Wayne plays what can best be described as a typical John Wayne role."

Otis L. Guernsey, Jr., *New York Herald Tribune*

John Wayne and Joanne Dru

John Wayne, Pedro Armendariz, and Harry Carey, Jr.

Three Godfathers

Argosy Picture Corporation

A METRO-GOLDWYN-MAYER PICTURE

CAST:

John Wayne, Pedro Armendariz, Harry Carey, Jr.,
Ward Bond, Mae Marsh, Mildred Natwick, Jane
Darwell, Guy Kibbee, Dorothy Ford, Ben Johnson,
Charles Halton, Hank Worden, Jack Pennick, Fred
Libby, Michael Dugan, Don Summers.

CREDITS:

Produced by John Ford and Merian C. Cooper. Directed by John Ford. Screenplay by Laurence Stallings
and Frank S. Nugent. Original story by Peter B. Kyne.

Photographed by Winton Hoch and Charles Boyle.
Color by Technicolor. Art director: James Basevi.

SYNOPSIS:

Three badmen, Robert Hightower (John Wayne),
Pete (Pedro Armendariz), and the Abilene Kid (Harry
Carey, Jr.) make their getaway in a hail of bullets
after robbing the bank of the frontier town of Wel-
come, Arizona. The gunfight shunts them out into the
desert wasteland. One of the bullets found its mark
in the arm of the Kid. But the badmen are tough
and desert-wise and they pit their skill and determina-

Pedro Armendariz and John Wayne

Harry Carey, Jr., Pedro Armendariz, and John Wayne

tion against their two most powerful enemies: the desert and United States Marshal Buck Sweet (Ward Bond) who loses pursuit of the three but not until a bullet pierces their waterbag.

The fugitives head for Mojave Wells, water take-on point for the railroad. When they arrive there, thirsty and tired, they see coming down the track on a flatcar, pulled by a locomotive, Buck Sweet and a posse.

The badmen summon their remaining strength and strike out over the desert again, this time heading for a subterranean spring.

En route they stop at a water hole and find a covered wagon stalled in the desert sand. The dried up water hole has been dynamited by the emigrant, who has gone off in search of water. Inside the cov-ered wagon the badmen discover an expectant mother. Pete delivers the baby, but the mother dies. The three badmen accept the dying woman's charge that they protect her baby. Deeply moved, they become the three godfathers.

They stumble on, their rough hands tender in the caring for the baby. The Kid, knowing he is about to die, reads the dead mother's Bible. Finally, he comes to the end of his strength. With a childhood prayer on his lips, he dies.

He leaves with his two pals the awareness of a dramatic parallel, which he points out in his last hours. It's almost Christmas Eve, they seem to be following a bright star in the desert night, they're carrying a baby, and their destination is Jerusalem—New Jerusalem, Arizona.

Pete is plodding ahead, holding the baby, when his foot goes into a gopher hole. To avoid falling headlong on the baby, Pete twists, breaking his leg. He comes to a sitting position. He and Bob make a crucial decision. Pete is left to die—Bob's remaining strength is used to get the baby to New Jerusalem. Bob gives his gun to Pete who shoots himself as Bob is walking off.

He arrives with his precious bundle on Christmas Eve. Almost falling through the door of the Last Chance Saloon as a melodeon plays "Holy Night."

Bob is tried and, although given a minimum sentence, his struggle to save the baby makes him the town hero. On the platform of the prison-bound train, Bob waves to the townspeople among whom he will soon raise his godson.

Running time: 106 minutes
Release date: December 1, 1948

[*REVIEW*]

"John Wayne as the leading badman and ultimate champion of the child is wonderfully raw and ructious. There is humor and honest tear-jerking in this visually beautiful film."

Bosley Crowther, *The New York Times*

"Wayne is better than ever as the leader of the badmen."

Howard Barnes, *New York Herald Tribune*

Guy Kibbee, John Wayne,
Ward Bond, and unidentified players

Adele Mara, John Wayne, and Gig Young

Wake of the Red Witch

REPUBLIC PICTURES

CAST:

John Wayne, Gail Russell, Gig Young, Adele Mara, Luther Adler, Eduard Franz, Grant Withers, Henry Daniell, Paul Fix, Dennis Hoey, Jeff Corey, Erskine Sanford, Duke Kahanamoku, Harry Brandon, John Wengraf, Myron Healey, Fred Libby.

CREDITS:

Associate producer: Edmund Grainger. Directed by Edward Ludwig. Screenplay by Harry Brown and Kenneth Gamet. Based on the novel *Wake of the Red Witch* by Garland Roark. Photographed by Reggie Lanning. Edited by Richard L. Van Enger. Art direction by James Sullivan. Music by Nathan Scott. Orchestrations by Stanley Wilson. Sound by T. A. Carman and Howard Wilson.

SYNOPSIS:

Sea Captain Ralls (John Wayne) deliberately sinks his ship, the Red Witch sailing vessel owned by Batjak, Ltd., Dutch East Indies Trading Company. The Maritime Commission investigation which ensues is halted abruptly by Mayrant Ruysdaal Sidneye (Luther Adler), wealthy and powerful head of Batjak.

Ralls, with his partner, Sam Rosen (Gig Young), and mate, Ripper (Paul Fix), sets out in an aged schooner, sailing in all sorts of weather—watching, waiting. Then finally come to a South Sea Island lagoon, ostensibly to hunt for pearls. Actually, a far

167

John Wayne and Gail Russell

richer treasure has drawn them to this part of the world. When they are welcomed by Sidneye, Sam soon becomes aware of the undercurrents of greed and passion which motivate the lives of Ralls and the trader. Sam falls in love with beautiful Teleia Van Schreeven (Adele Mara) who warns him of danger. Then Sidneye invites him to dinner and tells Sam a strange story.

Seven years before, the crew of Sidneye's schooner, the Red Witch, rescued Ralls from the shark infested waters around the Gilbert Islands. From the first meeting, the two were destined for a rivalry of titanic proportions, Sidneye had heard of the swashbuckling, wealth-seeking adventurer Ralls, and Ralls knew of the trader's ruthlessness and greed in propagating his fortune. They agreed to join forces in taking from the natives of a Polynesian island their fabulous fortune in pearls.

Arriving at Tahuata, both Ralls and Sidneye fell passionately in love with Angelique Desaix (Gail Russell), beautiful niece of the local French Commissaire (Henry Daniell). Ralls accomplished a sensational coup in persuading the natives of his divine right to take the pearls away to far corners of the earth after he wrested the coveted casket from the octopus which guarded its hiding place in a cave under the sea.

Gail Russell, John Wayne, Adele Mara, and Luther Adler

Horrified at Ralls' accidental killing of her uncle, Angelique agreed to marry Sidneye, though her heart was really with Ralls. Thus began the bitter, poisonous enmity between Ralls and Sidneye, each awaiting his chance to destroy the other. Both men eventually lost Angelique when she died of an incurable tropical disease which left Sidneye crippled.

With the end of Sidneye's tale, Sam is forced to realize why they have all converged on this spot. They are in the wake of the Red Witch, sunk with a cargo of millions in gold bullion. Ralls alone knows where she sank! Goaded by his desperate greed, Sidneye agrees to go fifty-fifty if Ralls will salvage the gold; he also agrees to allow Sam to take Teleia away.

Ralls loses his life while diving to bring up the sunken bullion when the Red Witch plunges from the ocean-bed shelf on which she is perched into the fathomless reaches of the Pacific. As Sidneye sits, broken in mind and body, staring down into the depths in which Ralls has vanished, Ralls' spirit, reunited with Angelique, sails away into the next world on the ghostly Red Witch.

Running time: 106 minutes
Release date: December 31, 1948

John Wayne and Luther Adler

Gail Russell and John Wayne

Joanne Dru and John Wayne

She Wore a Yellow Ribbon

An Argosy Production

RKO RADIO PICTURES

CAST:

John Wayne, Joanne Dru, John Agar, Ben Johnson, Harry Carey, Jr., Victor McLaglen, Mildred Natwick, George O'Brien, Arthur Shields, Harry Woods, Chief Big Tree, Noble Johnson, Cliff Lyons, Tom Tyler, Michael Dugan, Mickey Simpson, Frank McGrath, Don Summer, Fred Libby, Jack Pennick, Billy Jones, Fred Graham, Fred Kennedy, Rudy Bowman, Ray Hyke, Lee Bradley.

CREDITS:

Produced by John Ford and Merian C. Cooper. Directed by John Ford. Screenplay by Frank S. Nugent and Laurence Stallings. From the *Saturday Evening Post* story by James Warner Bellah. Photographed by Winton Hoch, ASC. Edited by Jack Murray. Art direction by James Basevi. Associate producer: Lowell Farrell. Second unit photography by Charles Boyle, ASC. Music by Richard Hageman. Assistant directors:

Wingate Smith and Edward O'Fearna. Sound by Frank
Webster and Clem Portman. Color by Technicolor.

SYNOPSIS:

Captain Brittles (John Wayne) has won the defer-
ence of his ranking officer, Major Allshard (George
O'Brien), respect from his junior officers, Lieutenants
Cohill (John Agar) and Pennell (Harry Carey, Jr.),
and affection from the men in the ranks such as
Sergeants Quincannon (Victor McLaglen) and Tyree
(Ben Johnson).

He has one last mission before returning to civil
life. The Indians have begun a holy war which he
must face. With his troop he leaves to trail them, but
at the same time must escort the Major's wife (Mildred Natwick) and her daughter Olivia (Joanne
Dru) out of the danger zone. Cohill and Pennell are
in love with Olivia, each vying to have her wear a
yellow ribbon as a token of his love. But at the stage
station they find it devastated and the residents mas-
sacred, and that all must return back with the women
to the fort.

On the return march, a scouting group witnesses
the fort's own sutler engaged in a deal with the Indians for repeating rifles. A quarrel ensues and the

Victor McLaglen and John Wayne

sutler and his men are slaughtered by the enraged braves, who then seize all the rifles.

As the column continues its march, moving parallel with it are a thousand warriors. Captain Brittles leaves behind a rear guard in order to gain time to get the women to the fort. There, Major Allshard relieves Captain Brittles of his command because of the latter's near termination of service. Under the command of Lt. Pennell, the troop fares forth again, imperilled by the overwhelming force of Indians. But Captain Brittles, realizing the inexperience of Lt. Pennell, overtakes the column, and takes over as the troop nears the encampment of the enemy.

Captain Brittles has formed a plan of campaign to avoid a hopeless battle. He rides boldly into the war camp of the Indians, ostensibly for a powwow with their leader, but really to scout the layout of their concentration. The powwow has no result, and the captain and his small escort barely get away with their lives.

Now his plan of action unfolds. The column at full gallop descends upon the encampment, firing wildly and stampeding hundreds of Indian ponies. The action puts the Indians afoot and they retreat to their reservations.

Just as Captain Brittles bids the fort farewell, word comes that he has been appointed Chief of Civilian Scouts with the rank of Brevet Lieutenant Colonel.

Running time: 104 minutes
Release date: July 28, 1949

REVIEW:

"In this big Technicolored Western, Mr. Ford has superbly achieved a vast and composite illustration of all the legends of the frontier cavalryman. Mr. Wayne, his hair streaked with silver and wearing a dashing mustache, is the absolute image and ideal of the legendary cavalryman."

Bosley Crowther, *The New York Times*

John Wayne and Victor McLaglen

The Fighting Kentuckian

REPUBLIC PICTURES

Vera Hruba Ralston, Oliver Hardy, and John Wayne

CAST:

John Wayne, Vera Ralston, Philip Dorn, Oliver Hardy, Marie Windsor, John Howard, Hugo Haas, Grant Withers, Odette Myrtil, Paul Fix, Mae Marsh, Jack Pennick, Mickey Simpson.

CREDITS:

Produced by John Wayne. Directed and written by George Waggner. Photographed by Lee Garmes, ASC. Edited by Richard L. Van Enger. Art direction by James Sullivan. Orchestration by R. Dale Butts. Special effects by Howard and Theodore Lydecker. Musical score by George Antheil. Costumes by Adele Palmer. Assistant director: Lee Lukather.

SYNOPSIS:

After Napoleon's defeat at Waterloo, his officers and their families, exiled from France, turned to America. By Act of Congress in 1817, they were granted four townships in the territory of Alabama, and they set out to carve homes out of the wilderness.

Led by such fine officers as Colonel Geraud (Philip Dorn) and General Marchand (Hugo Haas), the settlers struggle to bring order out of chaos and by the summer of 1819, the town of Demopolis is a thriving, bustling community.

On a shopping trip to Mobile, the general's lovely daughter, Fleurette (Vera Ralston), has a romantic introduction to rugged Kentucky rifleman, John Breen (John Wayne). Captivated by the girl's charm, Breen detours his regiment through Demopolis, and continues his ardent wooing of Fleurette.

Practicality must be the first concern of the De Marchands and Fleurette's mother (Odette Myrtil), though a romantic at heart, must suppress her sympathy with her daughter's desire to marry for love. She and the general must bow to the needs of their fellow exiles, and they are at the mercy of wealthy and powerful Blake Randolph (John Howard), who is determined to marry their daughter.

But Breen's independent American spirit rebels against the sacrifice of his and Fleurette's love. He resigns from his regiment and challenges the warnings issued by Randolph and the wily George Hayden (Grant Withers), who controls the rivermen. Supported by his cohort, Willie Paine (Oliver Hardy), Breen discovers evidence of a scheme Hayden, Ann Logan (Marie Windsor) and Beau Merritt (Paul Fix) have set up to evict the French settlers from their lands by switching the stakes set by the surveyors.

This plot evolves into a pitched battle between the French forces and the rivermen killers. Randolph is shot down in cold blood by Hayden when, for Fleurette's sake, he tries to halt the evictions. And Breen, after a roaring chase, shoots Hayden. Finally, the Second Kentucky Riflemen, led by General Andrew Jackson, come to the rescue. The rivermen are routed; the French colony is saved; and Breen marries Fleurette as the Fighting Kentuckians take to the trail once more.

Running time: 100 minutes
Release date: September 15, 1949

John Wayne and John Agar

Sands of Iwo Jima

REPUBLIC PICTURES

CAST:

John Wayne, John Agar, Adele Mara, Forrest Tucker, Wally Cassell, James Brown, Richard Webb, Arthur Franz, Julie Bishop, James Holden, Peter Coe, Richard Jaeckel, Bill Murphy, George Tyne, Hal Fieberling, John McGuire, Martin Milner, Leonard Gumley, William Self, Dorothy Ford, Dick Jones, David Clarke.

CREDITS:

Associate producer: Edmund Grainger. Directed by Allan Dwan. Screenplay by Harry Brown and James Edward Grant. Story by Harry Brown. Photographed by Reggie Lanning. Edited by Richard L. Van Enger. Music by Victor Young. Art direction by James Sullivan. Sound by T. A. Carman and Howard Wilson.

SYNOPSIS:

At Camp Packakariki, New Zealand, in 1943, a squad of U.S. Marines that is to make World War II history on the island of Iwo Jima learn to be fighters—from seasoned campaigner, Sergeant John M. Stryker (John Wayne).

Stryker's ruthless training tactics put hate into the hearts of his men. He has the dislike of all of them, but Pfc. Peter Conway (John Agar) detests the sergeant even more than the others do. Stryker has served Peter's father Colonel Sam Conway, who was killed at Guadalcanal four months before. Since Peter has taken a psychological beating all of his life from his father, who considered him soft, he doesn't go for Stryker's extravagant praise of the colonel. And Stryker tries to dissuade him from marrying Allison Bromley (Adele Mara) whom he meets at a servicemen's

174

club in Wellington. Peter rejects the advice. He receives permission to marry and has a short honeymoon before orders come to take off.

At Tarawa, the men Stryker has trained so thoroughly appreciate his fighting acumen. Up against Japan's best marines, Stryker and his leathernecks have to take an island that naval gunners and B-24's have been giving a workover for seventy-two days. Stryker risks his life to blow up a bunker full of Japs with a skillfully thrown satchel bomb.

In the course of the battle, one of Stryker's trainees, Handsome Dan Shipley (Richard Webb), is killed. Another, Choynski (Hal Fieberling), is hit by a sniper. And another, Hellenopolis (Peter Coe), dies when Corporal Thomas (Forrest Tucker), meeting an old Marine pal, stops for some coffee, while Hellenopolis waits for the ammunition which Thomas brings too late.

Conway, still resentful toward Stryker, tries rebelliously to rescue Bass (James Brown), Stryker's only friend, when he is left wounded in the line of fire. In spite of Bass' piteous cries, Stryker, more concerned with taking the island than with individuals, refuses to allow Conway to take the risk.

Finally, Tarawa is taken. The squad has a short leave in Hawaii and there Stryker has a brief experience with a street woman (Julie Bishop) that reveals the cause of his bitterness. His wife had left him years before, refusing to allow him to see his young son. The interlude softens Stryker, makes him more human, and by the time the squadron goes to Iwo Jima, even Conway is aware of the change.

In the desperate battle—to take an island of volcanic rock and lava—Conway becomes the fighter his father always hoped he would be. With Ragazzi (Wally Cassell and Conway, Stryker stages a three-way-play

with a grenade that destroys the Japs' hold on the island.

The famous flag-raising on Mt. Suribachi immortalizes the capture of Iwo Jima by the U.S. Marines. At the end of the battle, Stryker is shot by a Jap while smoking a cigarette. Conway kills the Jap, and now completely converted to his father's ideals, promises to name his son, recently born, after his famous father.

Running time: 109 minutes
Release date: December 14, 1949

John Wayne, Victor McLaglen, Maureen O'Hara, and J. Carrol Naish

Rio Grande

An Argosy Production

REPUBLIC PICTURES

CAST:

John Wayne, Maureen O'Hara, Ben Johnson, J. Carrol Naish, Victor McLaglen, Chill Wills, Harry Carey, Jr., Claude Jarman, Jr., Grant Withers, and The Sons of the Pioneers.

CREDITS:

Produced by John Ford and Merian C. Cooper. Directed by John Ford. Screenplay by James Kevin McGuiness. Based on a *Saturday Evening Post* story "Mission With No Record" by James Warner Bellah. Photographed by Bert Glennon, ASC. Second unit photography by A. J. Stout, ASC. Art direction by Frank Hotaling. Edited by Jack Murray. Music by Victor Young.

SYNOPSIS:

As an officer in the Union Army, under the command of General Sheridan (J. Carrol Naish), Lt. Col. Kirby Yorke (John Wayne) was obliged to burn the plantation of his Southern-born wife (Maureen O'Hara). She refused to forgive him and they have been estranged for fifteen years. During that time he has not seen his son, Jeff (Claude Jarman, Jr.).

Col. Yorke has thrown himself wholeheartedly into fighting the Indian Wars in the West—a lost cause since the U.S. and Mexican governments have

agreed that their military forces will not cross the Rio Grande under any circumstances. This enables the Apaches to raid, torture, kill the whites, then escape across the border and be safe from attack.

The situation is at a stalemate when General Sheridan arrives at Yorke's headquarters, on a routine inspection. Yorke is supposed to whip the Apaches into submission in order to make the Southwest safe for settlers, but the border sanctuary set-up and the shortage of troops have him licked. Thus, at the worst possible time, Yorke's son, Jeff, enlists in the army, having flunked out of West Point. He is assigned to his father's command as an ordinary trooper.

Then Mrs. Yorke arrives at the fort and, flaunting her charms before Yorke's love-starved eyes, she tries to obtain his agreement to young Jeff's discharge. Jeff and his father both hold out against her but she embarrasses them by taking her place among the enlisted men's wives and mothers on "laundresses' row."

A fresh attack by the Apaches leads General Sheridan to give Col. Yorke informal permission to cross the border and smoke the Indians out of their

Maureen O'Hara and John Wayne

hideout. They both know it will mean a court's martial for Yorke, but the General promises to handpick the members of the court.

The mission succeeds and the Apaches are taught a lesson. Jeff acquits himself admirably and by doing so cuts loose from his mother's domination. The colonel, as "punishment," is sent to the Court of St. James as U.S. military attaché. This pleases his wife immensely. They are reconciled and the trip to England serves as a second honeymoon.

Running time: 105 minutes
Release date: November 2, 1950

REVIEW:

"John Wayne turns in a first rate portrayal of a ramrod, wreckage and ruin Colonel estranged from his wife and compelled to send his son on a dangerous mission."

New York Herald Tribune

John Wayne, Maureen O'Hara, and Victor McLaglen

Claude Jarman, Jr., and John Wayne

John Wayne and Ward Bond

Operation Pacific

WARNER BROTHERS

CAST:

John Wayne, Patricia Neal, Ward Bond, Scott Forbes, Philip Carey, Martin Milner, Jack Pennick, Paul Picerni, Bill Campbell, Kathryn Givney, Virginia Brissac.

CREDITS:

Produced by Louis F. Edelman. Written and directed by George Waggner. Photographed by Bert Glennon, ASC. Edited by Alan Crosland, Jr. Art direction by Leo K. Kuter. Music by Max Steiner.

SYNOPSIS:

While aboard the U.S. submarine *Thunderfish,* on patrol off an enemy-held island, Ward Bond, the skipper, views Lt. Commander John Wayne, crashing out of the jungle with a baby in his arms. Safely on board, Wayns explains how he adopted the baby because it reminded him of his own son who died at infancy, revealing also that he is divorced from navy nurse Patricia Neal, whom he still loves.

Following a brief skirmish with opposing cruisers, the sub returns to the base where Wayne runs into

Pat, now dating Philip Carey, a navy pilot and Bond's younger brother. Off on another patrol *Thunderfish* is crippled by an armed decoy and Bond is wounded. Rather than risk the lives of the crew Wayne orders the craft to submerge, leaving the dying skipper behind.* Carey blames him for Bond's death, but Pat intervenes because she, too, still loves Wayne. It isn't until Wayne, in command of *Thunderfish* intercepts the battle line of the enemy armada, alerts the base and rescues a number of bailed-out pilots, among them Carey, that he and his crew are acclaimed heroes. As the sub returns from its victorious cruise, skipper Wayne sees Pat waiting for him.

Running time: 111 minutes
Release date: January 10, 1951

* Wrong! Bond orders the
sub to dive as he lays
dying on the conning tower.

Scott Forbes, Jack Morton, and John Wayne

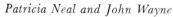
Patricia Neal and John Wayne

John Wayne, Robert Ryan, and William Harrigan

Flying Leathernecks

RKO RADIO PICTURES

CAST:

John Wayne, Robert Ryan, Don Taylor, Janis Carter, Jay C. Flippen, William Harrigan, James Bell, Barry Kelley, Maurice Jara, Adam Williams, James Dobson, Carleton Young, Steve Flagg, Brett King, Gordon Gebert.

CREDITS:

Presented by Howard Hughes. Produced by Edmund Grainger. Directed by Nicholas Ray. Screenplay by James Edward Grant. Original story by Kenneth Gamet. Photographed by William E. Snyder, ASC. Art direction by Albert D'Agostino and James W. Sullivan. Edited by Sherman Todd. Music by Roy Webb.

Sound by Frank McWhorter and Clem Portman. Color by Technicolor.

SYNOPSIS:

Major Dan Kirby (John Wayne), head of a Marine fighter squadron in the South Pacific is disliked by his men and his executive officer, Capt. Carl Griffin (Robert Ryan). Kirby is a strict disciplinarian and the men feel he is too hard on them. But the men learn that in the crucible of war, discipline is what stands between death and a chance to survive.

Running time: 102 minutes
Release date: July 18, 1951

Barry Fitzgerald, John Wayne, Ward Bond, and Victor McLaglen

The Quiet Man

An Argosy Production

A REPUBLIC PICTURE

CAST:

John Wayne, Maureen O'Hara, Barry Fitzgerald, Ward Bond, Victor McLaglen, Mildred Natwick, Francis Ford, Eileen Crowe, May Craig, Arthur Shields, Charles Fitzsimmons, James Lilburn, Sean Mc-Glory, Jack McGowran, Joseph O'Dea, Eric Gorman, Kevin Lawless, Paddy O'Donnell, Webb Overlander, Patrick Wayne, Michael Wayne, Melinda Wayne, Anthony Wayne.

CREDITS:

Produced by Merian C. Cooper. Directed by John Ford. Screenplay by Frank S. Nugent. Based on the story by Maurice Walsh. Photographed by Winton C. Hoch, ASC. Edited by Jack Murray, ACE. Music by Victor Young. Second unit photography by Archie Stout, ASC. Art direction by Frank Hotaling. Sound by T. A. Carman and Howard Wilcon. Color by Technicolor.

SYNOPSIS:

Sean Thornton (John Wayne), an American prizefighter returns to the village of Inisfree to settle down following his killing of a man in the ring. Peace is all he wants but with the purchase of White O'Mornin', the cottage where he was born, his troubles begin.

Burly Red Will Danaher (Victor McLaglen), the village bully who has plenty of land, covets that particular piece because it adjoins that of the rich widow Tillane (Mildred Natwick), whom he also covets.

Then Sean meets and falls in love with Danaher's pretty sister, Mary Kate (Maureen O'Hara), and the villagers gleefully wait for the fireworks. But they are sadly disappointed. Aided by the local priest, Father

John Wayne and Maureen O'Hara

Lonergan (Ward Bond), and one Michaeleen Flynn (Barry Fitzgerald), who acts as the village marriage broker when he isn't making book on the horses. Sean gets White O'Mornin' and he also gets Mary Kate without a single blow being exchanged.

The wedding is a charming affair that promises a bit of action when Danaher refuses to pay Mary Kate's rightful dowry but again Sean avoids a fight. White O'Mornin' is the scene of a honeymoon without love and filled with taunts and recriminations over Sean's cowardice and fear to fight Red Will for what is Mary Kate's, the dowry.

Under the taunts of his bride and the prompting of the villagers, Sean makes up his mind, but not before Mary Kate has left him and boarded the train for Dublin. Angry now and moved to action, Sean arrives on the double quick, yanks Mary Kate from the train, literally drags her across the station platform and heads afoot, straight for the Danaher farm.

When Sean hurls Mary Kate at her brother's feet, yelling, "no dowry, no marriage!" Danaher, for

John Wayne and Maureen O'Hara

the first time is at a loss, and shamed before the whole village by the return of his sister, promptly pays the money to Sean. That is one thing, but when Sean tosses the money into a nearby kiln, that is quite another. White with rage Red Will throws a ham-like fist into Sean's face.

And the fight is on! From Danaher's farm it ebbs and flows across the fields, over the meadows, through the brooks and takes its first breather in the village itself in a bar where combatants and onlookers alike have a bit of a refresher.

New wagers are laid and the second round begins when Sean knocks Red Will through the side wall of the pub. Over the cobbled streets of Inisfree the fight sways back and forth until both fall exhausted and unconquered, but with a new respect for each other. At last, peace and quiet comes to Inisfree and to Sean and his bride, Mary Kate, and their love nest, White O'Mornin'.

Running time: 129 minutes
Release date: May 12, 1952

Barry Fitzgerald and John Wayne

John Wayne and Victor McLaglen

Nancy Olson, John Wayne, and John Hubbard

Big Jim McLain

A Wayne-Fellows Production

WARNER BROTHERS

CAST:

John Wayne, Nancy Olson, James Arness, Alan Napier, Gayne Whitman, Hans Conreid, Veda Ann Borg, Hal Baylor, Robert Keys, John Hubbard, Sarah Padden, Dan Liu.

CREDITS:

Produced by Robert Fellows. Directed by Edward Ludwig. Screenplay by James Edward Grant, Richard English and Eric Taylor. Based on a story by Richard English. Photographed by A. J. Stout, ASC. Edited by Jack Murray, ACE. Art direction by Al Ybarra. Musical direction by Emil Newman. Assistant director: Andrew V. McLaglen.

SYNOPSIS:

Big Jim McLain (John Wayne), special agent, and his assistant Mal Baxter (James Arness) are assigned to investigate the nefarious activities of a world-wide* terror ring with headquarters in Hawaii. While checking on suspect Dr. Gelster (Gayne Whitman), Jim meets and falls in love with the psychiatrist's secretary, Nancy Vallon (Nancy Olson). From a local character,

186

* I.e., the Communist Party

McLain and his aide discover the name of the man who is the contact for the terrorists. They get a key to his home, question the landlady and are rewarded with names of the top leaders—some of them high in social circles. Following fruitless leads which take him into a Shinto Temple, public bath houses and remote parts of the islands, Jim decides to use an old police trick to smoke out his adversaries. At a party, he lets it be known that he has uncovered the names of some important people who are involved in the plot. Jim also promises an early arrest of the head man. The ruse works too well. Mal is blackjacked and brought to Dr. Gelster who, in administering an overdose of truth serum, kills the investigator. Bent on revenge, Jim, with the help of the Honolulu police, ferrets out and smashes the ring. Mal's killer captured, Jim is free to marry Nancy.

Running time: 90 minutes
Release date: September 3, 1952

James Arness and John Wayne

Nancy Olson and John Wayne

John Wayne and Donna Reed

Trouble Along the Way

WARNER BROTHERS

CAST:

John Wayne, Donna Reed, Charles Coburn, Tom Tully, Marie Windsor, Sherry Jackson, Tom Helmore, Dabbs Greer, Leif Erickson, Douglas Spencer, Chuck Connors.

CREDITS:

Produced by Melville Shavelson. Directed by Michael Curtiz. Screenplay by Melville Shavelson and Jack Rose. Story by Douglas Morrow and Robert Hardy Andrews. Photographed by A. J. Stout, ASC. Edited by Ownes Marks. Art direction by Leo K. Kuter. Music by Max Steiner.

SYNOPSIS:

Father Burke (Charles Coburn), rector of St. Anthony's College, is informed that the school will be closed down in six months unless he can raise $170,000, the amount for which the college is in debt. Seeking to raise the money through St. Anthony's football team, Burke approaches one-time coach Steve Williams (John Wayne) with an offer which Steve refuses. Later, Steve is confronted by Alice Singleton (Donna Reed), a probation officer who is investigating a complaint by his ex-wife that he is neglecting his daughter Carol (Sherry Jackson). This move brings Steve to accept Burke's proposition to coach the team. He and Carol arrive at St. Anthony's, but find the athletic facilities in terrible shape. Steve sends for two of his former associates, and together they begin the hard task of rebuilding the football team.

After a grueling summer session of football, St. Anthony's is ready to roll against Santa Carla. The big game, and Steve's team wins, but the coach's happiness is short-lived. He has a falling out with Father Burke and his ex-wife starts court proceedings for Carol's custody. Alice, in love with Steve, testifies in his behalf. Meanwhile, Carol is ordered to the custody of the Children's Center. As Alice and Carol leave for the shelter, Father Burke offers to be a character witness for Steve at the next hearing, and promises Steve his coaching job at St. Anthony's next season. Carol gives her dad the high sign that Alice is okay with her. Steve agrees and there isn't much doubt that Carol will have a new mother soon.

Running time: 110 minutes
Release date: March 18, 1953

Sherry Jackson and John Wayne

Charles Coburn and John Wayne

Wally Cassell, Hal Baylor, John Wayne, Sean McGlory, and unidentified player

Island in the Sky

A Wayne-Fellows Production

WARNER BROTHERS

CAST:

John Wayne, Lloyd Nolan, Walter Abel, James Arness, Andy Devine, Allyn Joslyn, James Lydon, Harry Carey, Jr., Hal Baylor, Sean McGlory, Wally Cassell, Gordon Jones, Frank Fenton, Robert Keys, Sumner Getchell, Regis Toomey, Paul Fix, Jim Dugan, George Chandler, Bob Steele, Darryl Hickman, Touch Connors, Carl Switzer, Cass Gidley, Guy Anderson.

CREDITS:

Directed by William A. Wellman. Screenplay by Ernest K. Gann, from his novel *Island in the Sky*. Photographed by A. J. Stout, ASC. Aerial photography by William Clothier. Edited by Ralph Dawson, ACE.

Art direction by James Basevi. Assistant director: Andrew V. McLaglen. Production manager: Nate H. Edwards. Music by Emil Newman.

SYNOPSIS:

Dooley (John Wayne), one of a veteran group of civilian pilots flying for the Army Transport Command, is in trouble aloft with his crew of four. Ice weighs his C-47's wings and he skillfully brings his plane down—in 40° below uncharted Labrador territory. Back at headquarters Col. Fuller (Walter Abel), assembles Dooley's pilot buddies, Moon, McMullen, Stutz, Handy (Andy Devine, James Arness, Lloyd Nolan, Allyn Joslyn), all of whom, weary from just-finished flights or at home with their families, rally to the search for one of their number. The search, in bad weather and good, over lands where most navigational aids work trickily or not at all, commences.

Dooley proves his hardiness by keeping his crew together, all except his co-pilot, Lovatt (Sean McGlory), who wanders off but a few yards in a storm hunting for live game, and is lost to the elements. The men under Dooley utilize their resourcefulness in sending bearing signals with their remaining battery strength until that, too, is gone. The intrepid pilots in the air are sighted and fly almost overhead but heartbreakingly miss the little group on the ground. Fuel almost exhausted, they return to base. With the search in its sixth day, the planes again out, Dooley's radioman sends a signal with an emergency radio and a fix is gotten—the planes home in on it—the downed fliers are sighted, food is dropped. The flying rescuers wheel and roar overhead one after another waving to their buddies on the ground.

Running time: 109 minutes
Release date: March 18, 1953

Sean McGlory and John Wayne

John Wayne, Geraldine Page, Tom Irish, and Ward Bond

Hondo

A Wayne-Fellows Production
WARNER BROTHERS

CAST:

John Wayne, Geraldine Page, Ward Bond, Michael Pate, Lee Aaker, James Arness, Rodolfo Acosta, Leo Gordon, Tom Irish, Paul Fix, Rayford Barnes.

CREDITS:

Produced by Robert Fellows. Directed by John Farrow. Screenplay by James Edward Grant. Based on the story by Louis L'Amour. Photographed by Robert Burks, ASC. and A. J. Stout, ASC. Edited by Ralph Dawson. Art direction by Al Ybarra. Music by Emil Newman and Hugo Friedhofer. Color by Warnercolor.

SYNOPSIS:

Riding dispatch for the U.S. Cavalry in the southwest of 1874, Hondo Lane (John Wayne) and his surly dog Sam come upon a lonely ranch tended by Angie Lowe (Geraldine Page) and her small son Johnny (Lee Aaker). During his brief stay, Hondo learns that Angie's husband Ed Lowe (Leo Gordon), has deserted her in the wake of an Apache uprising, yet she refuses to accompany Hondo to safety. After he rides off alone, Angie and her son are confronted by an Indian raiding party led by Vittorio (Michael Pate). When Silva (Rodolfo Acosta), second in command, approaches Johnny, the boy shoots at the Indian, creasing Silva's skull. This so impresses Vittorio, that he declares Johnny a blood brother and promises the Apaches will bother them no more.

At the frontier post, Hondo is informed that the Apaches are on the move, burning and murdering throughout the territory. At the post, Hondo runs into Lowe, and they exchange a few bitter words. Hondo decides to ride to the Lowe ranch and bring back Angie and Johnny. On the way, he is ambushed by Lowe and his partner. Hondo kills Lowe and then he is surrounded and captured by the Apaches. It is only after Hondo kills Lowe that he finds out who he is—when he finds a photo of Johnny on the dead body.

John Wayne and Geraldine Page

Hondo is brought to Vittorio, where Silva orders Hondo tortured. Though undergoing great pain, Hondo refuses to cry out. Vittorio, admiring his courage, orders him released, but to keep the peace with the protesting Silva, orders a knife duel between them. Hondo defeats Silva but spares his life. Hondo is delivered to the Lowe ranch, where he explains to Angie that he has killed her husband. Angie is saddened but her love for Hondo is stronger than it ever was for Lowe. She forgives him and they begin to plan for a future in California, where Hondo owns some land.

After Vittorio's death, Silva is chief, and he leads the Apaches in merciless assaults. Even the U.S. Cavalry is helpless. However, during a bitter siege of a wagon train led by Hondo, Silva is killed, and the Indians retreat. Hondo, Angie and Johnny are able to continue on their way to California.

Running time: 84 minutes
Release date: November 27, 1953

John Wayne, Rudolfo Acosta,
and Michael Pate

Jan Sterling, David Brian, Claire Trevor, John Wayne, John Smith and Karen Sharpe

The High and the Mighty

A Wayne-Fellows Produlction

WARNER BROTHERS

CAST:

John Wayne, Claire Trevor, Laraine Day, Robert Stack, Jan Sterling, Phil Harris, Robert Newton, David Brian, Paul Kelly, Sidney Blackmer, Julie Bishop, Pedro Gonzales-Gonzales, John Howard, Wally Brown, William Campbell, Ann Doran, John Qualen, Paul Fix, George Chandler, Joy Kim, Michael Wellman, Douglas Fowley, Regis Toomey, Carl Switzer, Robert Keys, William DeWolf Hopper, William Schallert, Julie Mitchum, Karen Sharpe, John Smith, Doe Avedon.

CREDITS:

Directed by William A. Wellman. Screenplay by Ernest K. Gann, from his novel *The High and the Mighty*.

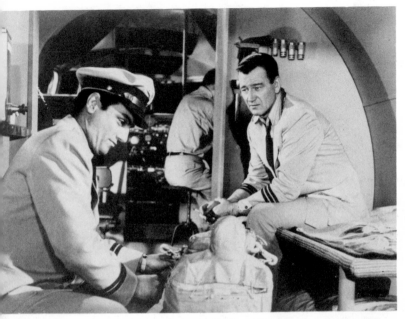

William Campbell and John Wayne

Photographed by A. J. Stout, ASC. Aerial photography by William Clothier. Edited by Ralph Dawson, ACE. Art direction by Al Ybarra. Special effects by Robert Mattey. Music composed and conducted by Dimitri Tiomkin. Production manager: Nate H. Edwards. Assistant director: Andrew V. McLaglen. Color by Warnercolor. Filmed in CinemaScope.

SYNOPSIS:

A Trans-Orient-Pacific Airlines plane takes off from Honolulu carrying a bizarre group of people: Dan Roman (John Wayne), co-pilot, a man who has used up his nine lives and was starting on his tenth; a host of beautiful women, Sally McKee (Jan Sterling), May Holst (Claire Trevor), Nell Buck (Karen Sharpe), Lydia Rice (Laraine Day), Ken Childs (David Brian) a wealthy collector of other people's wives, and an assortment of returning tourists.

John Wayne and Robert Stack

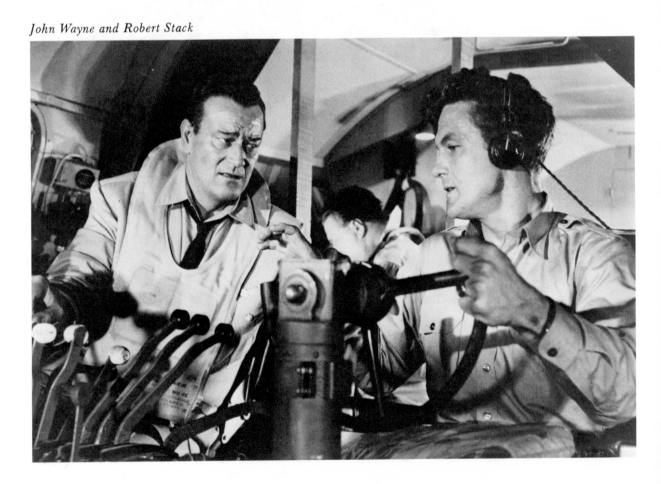

196

The plane wings towards its destination while, in the cabin, Lydia quarrels with her husband. Suddenly Agnew (Sidney Blackmer), brooding and sinister, accuses Childs of wife-stealing, and confronts the latter with a gun. As the other passengers rush to Childs' rescue, there is a burst of noise and the whole plane lurches violently. One of the motors, set ablaze, is shaken loose to dangle crazily from the wing.

With pilot Sullivan (Robert Stack) hysterical, Dan takes over, orders cargo and baggage thrown overboard to lighten the ship. Then Dan learns there is the barest of chances that they can reach the San Francisco airport if the scant gasoline holds out. From his co-pilot's stubborn determination, Sullivan gains new courage, as do the passengers whose lives have taken a bright turn for the best, after the perilous journey. Barely clearing the San Francisco hills, Sullivan brings his plane down at the airport—a routine landing.

Running time: 147 minutes
Release date: July 3, 1954

John Wayne and George Chandler

John Wayne, Laraine Day, John Howard, Julie Bishop, and Jan Sterling

John Wayne, Lana Turner, and Lyle Bettger

The Sea Chase

CAST:

John Wayne, Lana Turner, David Farrar, Lyle Bettger, Tab Hunter, James Arness, Richard Davalos, John Qualen, Paul Fix, Lowell Gilmore, Luis Van Rooten, Alan Hale, Wilton Graff, Peter Whitney, Claude Akins, John Doucette, Alan Lee.

CREDITS:

Produced and directed by John Farrow. Screenplay by James Warner Bellah and John Twist. From the novel by Andrew Geer. Photographed by William Clothier. Edited by William Ziegler. Art direction by Franz Bachelin. Music by Roy Webb. Orchestrations by Maurice de Packh and Leonid Raab. Sound by Francis J. Scheid. Assistant directors: Emmett Emerson and Russell Llewellyn. Color by Warnercolor. Filmed in CinemaScope.

SYNOPSIS:

Under cover of a heavy fog, an outlaw freighter, commanded by Captain Karl Ehrlich (John Wayne), slips out of Sydney harbor bound for Valparaiso. Among the passengers and crew are Elsa Keller (Lana Turner), in love with Ehrlich; first mate Kirchner (Lyle Bettger); mates Wesser (Tab Hunter) and Stemme (Richard Davalos). Hunted by Commander Napier (David Farrar) on board the British warship

198

The Sea Chase

The account given in the synopsis of what happens after the ship leaves Valparaiso is entirely inaccurate.

Knowing that Ehrlich will be heading for Europe, Napier requests and receives a North Sea command, where he does catch Ehrlich's ship. Ehrlich gives the log to a crew member, instructing him to deliver it to Napier. He then sends the entire crew w/ the exception of Kirchner into the lifeboats. Against Ehrlich's orders, Elsa stays behind with him and Napier subsequently sinks the ship. The viewer is left wondering whether or not Ehrlich and Elsa make it to the nearby Norwegian coast.

Rockhampton, Ehrich sends a detail ashore to raid a shipwreck station on Auckland Island for food and clothing. Six fishermen marooned there, are machine-gunned by Kirchner acting without orders. When *Rockhampton* touches Auckland, Napier's one-time admiration for Ehrlich turns to vengeful hatred.

Following a series of mishaps including the death of Stemme during an attack by sharks, Ehrlich's craft reaches Valparaiso. Refuelled and repaired, the freighter puts out to sea again, masquerading as a Panamanian banana boat. However, Napier penetrates the disguise and intercepts the ship. A furious battle rages. Sunk by British shells, the renegade vessel goes down with Ehrlich and Elsa. On the lifeboat that gets away, Elsa has managed to stow the log which reveals in Kirchner's own handwriting that Ehrich was innocent of the Auckland incident.

Running time: 117 minutes
Release date: May 12, 1955

✳ See notes.

John Wayne, Lauren Bacall, and Mike Mazurki

Blood Alley

A Batjac Production

WARNER BROTHERS

CAST:

John Wayne, Lauren Bacall, Paul Fix, Joy Kim, Berry Kroeger, Mike Mazurki, Anita Ekberg, Henry Nakamura, W. T. Chang, George Chan.

CREDITS:

Directed by William A. Wellman. Screenplay by A. S. Fleischman, from his novel *Blood Alley*. Photographed by William H. Clothier. Edited by Fred MacDowell.

Production designed by Alfred Ybarra. Music by Roy Webb. Orchestrations by Maurice de Packh and Gus Levene. Assistant director: Andrew V. McLaglen. Sound by Earl Crain, Sr. Color by Warnercolor. Filmed in CinemaScope.

SYNOPSIS:

Wilder (John Wayne), an adventurous merchant marine captain who knows every current, port and prevailing wind in the Far East, is approached by the

John Wayne and Lauren Bacall

John Wayne and Mike Mazurki

oppressed villagers of Chiku Shan. Led by lovely Cathy Grainger (Lauren Bacall), daughter of an American doctor in enemy occupied China, they want Wilder to guide their ship through "Blood Alley"—Formosa Straits—to Hong Kong and freedom. Impressed with the audacity of their plan and charmed by Cathy's beauty, Wilder agrees to the assignment. Following several skirmishes with enemy troops, the villagers board their craft and embark upon a dangerous journey. Once within bounds of Blood Alley the craft is pursued by a patrol boat which strikes a cleverly prepared trap and is sunk. An enemy plane buzzes them. Wilder, inspired by a tremendous flock of sea gulls hovering about the boat, orders the deck scattered with food. Momentarily, the gulls cover the ship as much as some of the reefs nearby. The plane passes. Almost within sight of their goal, they are intercepted by a destroyer, and bombarded. However, Wilder's able leadership brings them steaming into Hong Kong harbor with a minimum of casualties, though there is a gaping hole in the side and the stack is leaking smoke like a sieve. The ship is proud—and she is free. In port, Wilder declares his love for Cathy who admits she has been in love with him from the first.

Running time: 118 minutes
Release date: September 23, 1955

John Wayne and Lauren Bacall

Susan Hayward and John Wayne

The Conqueror

RKO RADIO PICTURES

CAST:

John Wayne, Susan Hayward, Pedro Armendariz, Agnes Moorehead, Thomas Gomez, John Hoyt, William Conrad, Ted de Corsia, Leslie Bradley, Leo Gordon, Lee Van Cleef, Peter Mamakos, Fred Graham, Richard Loo, George E. Stone, Jeanne Gerson, Lane Bradford, Sylvia Lewis.

CREDITS:

Presented by Howard Hughes. Produced and directed by Dick Powell. Written by Oscar Millard. Associate producer: Richard Sokolove. Photographed by Joseph LaShelle, ASC, Leo Tover, ASC, Harry J. Wild, ASC, and William Snyder, ASC. Editorial supervision by Stuart Gilmore, ACE. Edited by Robert Ford and Kenneth Marstella. Art direction by Albert D'Agostino and Carroll Clark. Music by Victor Young. Photographic effects by Linwood Dunn and Albert Simpson. Sound by Bernard Freericks and Terry Kellum. Color by Technicolor. Filmed in CinemaScope.

SYNOPSIS:

Temujin (John Wayne), his blood brother Jamuga (Pedro Armendariz) and his Mongols attack a Merkit caravan and capture Bortai (Susan Hayward), daugh-

John Wayne and Pedro Armendariz

ter of the Tartar ruler Kumlek. Temujin's mother and Jamuga, fearing Kumlek's wrath, beg him to set Bortai free but Temujin refuses. The Merkits storm Temujin's camp to rescue Bortai. They are defeated but Bortai escapes. Giving chase, Temujin recaptures her and declares he will make her his wife.

Temujin rallies his followers in a plan to get the mighty Chinese ruler, Wang Khan, to join forces in wiping out the Tartars. With the aid of the Khan's treacherous Shaman, he gains the Khan's approval, but before Temujin can put the plan into effect, he is wounded and Bortai rescued. Jamuga, attempting to aid Temujin, leads the Tartars to his hiding place. Kumlek sentences Temujin to death, but Bortai, realizing she loves him, sets him free.

Temujin, convinced by the Shaman that the Khan will doublecross him, captures the Khan's city, takes over as ruler of all the Mongols. In a terrific battle, he defeats the Tartars. Temujin, now the mighty Genghis Khan, and Bortai, his bride, prepare to take their place in history.

Running time: 110 minutes
Release date: February 21, 1956

Susan Hayward and Leo Gordon

John Wayne and Ted DeCorsia

John Wayne and Jeffrey Hunter

The Searchers

C. V. Whitney Picture
WARNER BROTHERS

CAST:

John Wayne, Jeffrey Hunter, Vera Miles, Natalie Wood, John Qualen, Olive Carey, Henry Brandon, Ken Curtis, Harry Carey, Jr., Antonio Moreno, Hank Worden, Lana Wood, Walter Coy, Dorothy Jordan, Pippa Scott, Pat Wayne, Beulah Archuletta, Ward Bond.

CREDITS:

Executive producer: Merian C. Cooper. Associate producer: Patrick Ford. Directed by John Ford. Screenplay by Frank S. Nugent. From the novel by Alan LeMay. Photographed by Winton C. Hoch, ASC.

Edited by Jack Murray. Sound by Hugh McDowell and Howard Wilson. Art direction by Frank Hotaling and James Basevi. Second unit photography by Alfred Gilhs, ASC. Special effects by George Brown. Production supervisor: Lowell J. Farell. Music by Max Steiner. Orchestration by Murray Cutter. The song, "The Searchers" by Stan Jones. Assistant director: Wingate Smith. Color by Technicolor.

SYNOPSIS:

Ethan Edwards (John Wayne) has come home to the Texas ranch he owns with his brother. He is warmly greeted by the family, and the next day they are joined by a band of Texas Rangers led by the Rev. Sam Clayton (Ward Bond), who are looking for cattle rustlers. Believing Indians responsible for the rustling, Ethan persuades his brother (Walter Coy) to remain with the family and he joins the posse with Martin Pawley (Jeffrey Hunter), a ward of the Edwards' since the massacre of his family by the Comanches. Finding that the Comanches had stolen the cattle only to draw the Rangers away from their homes, Ethan and Martin race back to the ranch. They find the family killed by Chief Scar's (Henry Brandon) raiders and realizing the youngest child, Debbie (Natalie Wood), and teenaged Lucy (Pippa Scott) have been carried off. Ethan, Martin and Brad Jorgensen (Harry Carey, Jr.), Lucy's boy friend, set out after the Indians. Days later Ethan finds the body of Lucy. At the news of her death Brad goes berserk with grief and single-handedly attacks the Comanche village where he is killed. Ethan and Martin continue in search of the girl until the snows of winter force them to turn back to the Jorgensen ranch where Laurie (Vera Miles) openly declares her love for Martin. She tries to stop him joining the determined Ethan in his search for Debbie, but he will not stop. The two searchers start out once more and though the months turn to years the two men continue to track the Comanches.

Walter Coy, John Wayne, Dorothy Jordan, and players

Friends and enemies alike offer information to Ethan but five years slip by before his first contact is made with the bloodthirsty Chief Scar.

In the New Mexican territory Ethan and Martin are led to the Indian's camp as traders. They find Debbie only to learn that she has grown to young womanhood as an Indian. Scar recognizes the two men and in the fight that follows, Ethan is badly wounded, and Martin takes him home. The scene they come upon is the marriage of Laurie to a young rancher (Ken Curtis), which Martin promptly breaks up in a rough-and-tumble fight. The fight is interrupted by Lt. Greenhill (Pat Wayne) of the cavalry who wants the Rangers to join them in action against Scar's band of Comanches. Ethan sees a chance to kill Debbie, whom he feels has disgraced the family by becoming a Comanche and volunteers to lead the Rangers. Martin slips into the Indian camp and kills Scar, but in the cavalry charge the Indians are routed and Ethan corners his niece. Faced with the prospect of killing the last of his own family, he relents and takes the child back to be raised by the Jorgensens.

Running time: 119 minutes
Release date: March 13, 1956

REVIEW:

"Wayne is fascinating for his sheer hardness. There's no kindness in his nature—he is crafty and arrogant and his eyes are cold as ice."
William K. Zinsser, *New York Herald Tribune*

John Wayne, player, and Jeffrey Hunter

John Wayne and Pat Wayne

John Wayne, Maureen O'Hara, and Dan Dailey

The Wings of Eagles

METRO-GOLDWYN-MAYER

CAST:

John Wayne, Dan Dailey, Maureen O'Hara, Ward Bond, Ken Curtis, Edmund Lowe, Kenneth Tobey, James Todd, Barry Kelley, Sig Ruman, Henry O'Neill, Willis Bouchey, Dorothy Jordan, Peter Ortiz, Louis Jean Heydt, Tige Andrews, Dan Borzage, William Tracy, Harlan Warde, Jack Pennick, Bill Henry, Mimi Gibson, Evelyn Rudie, Mae Marsh.

CREDITS:

Produced by Charles Schnee. Directed by John Ford. Associate producer: James E. Newcom. Screenplay by Frank Fenton and William Wister Haines. Based on the life and writings of Commander Frank W. (Spig) Wead. Photographed by Paul C. Vogel, ASC. Edited by Gene Ruggiero, ACE. Art direction by William A. Horning and Malcolm Brown. Special effects by Arnold Gillespie and Warren Newcombe. Assistant director: Wingate Smith. Music score by Jeff Alexander. Color by Metrocolor.

SYNOPSIS:

In 1919, the aviation branch of the U.S. Navy consisted of exactly twelve planes and thirty men. In an effort to dramatize its interest in aviation in order to win public support for congressional appropriations, the navy stages international seaplane races, and in 1923, the famous Schneider Cup is won by Annapolis graduate Frank (Spig) Wead (John Wayne) and his team. Then Wead and his friend Lt. John Price (Ken Curtis) in quick succession shatter the seaplane endurance record, set a new seaplane distance record and break the seaplane speed record. But Wead's passionate interest in naval aviation leads to a break with his wife, Minnie (Maureen O'Hara), who feels that he is neglecting her.

On the night that Wead receives word of his appointment as skipper of a fighter squadron, he breaks his neck in a fall down the stairs of his home. He is given up as a hopeless paraplegic by the doctors. Wead persuades Minnie to leave him and live her own life with their children. Nursed back to health by his old navy mechanic, Sgt. Carson (Dan Dailey), he begins a new career as an author, playwright and screen

Kenneth Tobey and John Wayne

Ward Bond and John Wayne

writer, dealing with the subject closest to his heart—aviation. At the height of his success, he and Minnie, now a successful business woman, plan to make another try at marriage, when the radio brings them the news that Pearl Harbor has been bombed by the Japanese.

Wead is sent to the Pacific to put into effect his revolutionary idea for jeep carriers to follow up the big carriers and replace lost planes, a plan which he sees successfully carried out at Kwajalein. But the arduous toil of the still partially crippled Wead takes its toll and after the battle he collapses. While the carrier's crew line the deck to pay him tribute, Wead, battered but far from beaten, is hoisted via breeches buoy to a destroyer for the last trip home. His long fight to win a strong air arm for the Navy has been won.

Running time: 118 minutes
Release date: January 30, 1957

John Wayne and Maureen O'Hara

Jet Pilot

An RKO RADIO PICTURE

Released by Universal-International

CAST:

John Wayne, Janet Leigh, Jay C. Flippen, Paul Fix, Richard Rober, Roland Winters, Hans Conreid, Ivan Triesault, John Bishop, Perdita Chandler, Joyce Compton, Denver Pyle, and the United States Air Force.

CREDITS:

Presented by Howard Hughes. Produced and written by Jules Furthman. Directed by Josef von Sternberg. Music by Bronislau Kaper. Photographed by Winton C. Hoch, ASC. Supervision of aerial sequences: Philip

John Wayne and Bill Erwin

G. Cochran. Assistant to the producer: Brig. Gen. Clarence A. Shoop. Art direction by Albert S. D'Agostino and Field Gray. Edited by Michael R. McAdam, Harry Marker, ACE, William M. Moore. Sound by Earl Wolcott and Terry Kellum. Color by Technicolor.

SYNOPSIS:

When a Russian jet lands at a U.S. air base in Alaska, Col. Shannon (John Wayne) is amazed to discover that the pilot is a woman (Janet Leigh), a Lieutenant in the Russian Air Force. She says she escaped from Russia to avoid being shot for disobedience, but Shannon doubts her story and flies her to Palmer Field for interrogation by Gen. Black (Jay C. Flippen).

Shannon is assigned by Washington to take her under his wing, to fly certain jet planes with her and to introduce her to the luxuries of American life in an

Janet Leigh and John Wayne

effort to get information on Soviet air power from her. Since she is blonde, beautiful and speaks English perfectly, Shannon naturally falls in love with her.

Washington decides that she is not going to give away any important secrets from her side of the Iron Curtain, and decides to jail her. This inspires Shannon to marry her, not knowing she is a spy. But when he learns that she doesn't love him for himself but only for his information, he enters a counter-conspiracy. The two of them escape to Russia in order to avoid the jail sentence.

In Siberia and later in Moscow, the wife discovers she really loves Shannon and that he really loves her. They decide to fly back to the U.S. They naturally steal a Russian jet and fly back to the U.S. with a host of secret information.

Running time: 112 minutes
Release date: September 23, 1957

Janet Leigh and John Wayne

John Wayne and Sophia Loren

Legend of the Lost

A Batjac Production, Panama, Inc. Presentation

UNITED ARTISTS

CAST:

John Wayne, Sophia Loren, Rossano Brazzi, Kurt Kasznar, Sonia Moser, Angela Portaluri, Ibrahim El Hadish.

CREDITS:

Produced and directed by Henry Hathaway. Screenplay by Robert Presnell, Jr. and Ben Hecht. Photographed by Jack Cardiff. Edited by Bert Bates. Music composed and conducted by A. F. Lavagnino. Art direction by Alfred Ybarra. Sound by John Keen and W. H. Milner. Color by Technicolor. Filmed in Technirama.

SYNOPSIS:

Paul Bonnard (Rossano Brazzi), a stranger on the streets of Timbuctoo, roams about the colorful market place seeking a guide to take him on a long trek into the Sahara. He approaches the fat and fatuous Prefect

Dukas (Kurt Kasznar), who is leading a funeral procession, regarding his quest. Dukas tells him of the foremost desert guide in the land—Joe January (John Wayne). The two meet and plan the perilous mission. Dita (Sophia Loren), a ravishing slave girl, is so taken by the mysterious stranger that she begs him to take her along. He refuses, but they find her on the desert with a band of native Tauregs. Paul allows her to join them against his guide's will. Paul tells Joe and Dita he is seeking a fabulous treasure at a lost city discovered by his father, an archeologist.

Fighting their way across the blistering sands they encounter another band of hostile Tauregs, a blinding sand storm and other seemingly insurmountable obstacles. Romantic nights under the desert stars launch a rivalry between the two men for Dita's affections. With their water supply running out and no signs of an oasis on the horizon, Joe starts to turn back, but almost immediately they discover the ruins of the lost city, Timgad, where Paul finds proof of an unsavory incident in the life of his father, whom he worshipped

Sophia Loren and John Wayne

John Wayne and Rossano Brazzi

as a saint. When the fabulous treasure of gold and gems is found, Paul attempts to attack Dita and kill Joe, a complete metamorphosis in his personality as a result of his lost faith in his father. Joe protects Dita and she realizes it is he whom she loves. Paul flees to the desert alone during the night, with all the supplies, donkeys and the treasure.

Joe and Dita trail Paul across the desert on foot and find him delirious from heat and exposure. They are near a dry river bed and as a last resort to prevent dying of thirst Joe starts to dig for water. As he is bending to his task Paul plunges a knife into his back, but before he can strike a fatal blow he is shot by Dita and dies. Dita and Joe lie on the flaming sands, knowing they will soon die of thirst. Their faith and newly found love is all they have. Suddenly a great cloud of dust rolls across the desert. It is a camel caravan, headed for civilization, and the seemingly doomed couple discover a new life.

Running time: 109 minutes
Release date: December 17, 1957

Sophia Loren and John Wayne

Angie Dickinson and John Wayne

I Married a Woman

RKO RADIO PICTURES

Released by Universal-International

CAST:

George Gobel, Diana Dors, Adolphe Menjou, Jessie Royce-Landis, Nita Talbot, William Redfield, Steve Dunne, John McGiver, Steve Pendleton, Cheerio Meredith, Kay Buckley, Angie Dickinson and John Wayne.

CREDITS:

Produced by William Bloom. Directed by Hal Kanter. Written by Goodman Ace. Photographed by Lucien Ballard, ASC. Edited by Kenneth Marstella. Art direction by Albert S. D'Agostino and Walter E. Keller. Sound by Frank Webster and Terry Kellum. Music by Cyril Mockridge. Assistant director: John E. Pommer.

SYNOPSIS:

Marshall Briggs (George Gobel), wizard of the Sutton Advertising Agency, must come up with a fast idea to follow his terrific "Miss Luxenberg" beauty contest or the firm will lose its top account—Luxenberg Beer.

He comes up with the "Mrs. Luxenberg" contest and the previous Miss Luxenberg (Diana Dors), now married to Marshall wins the "Mrs. Luxenberg" title.

John Wayne portrays Diana Dors' favorite movie star and is seen in several scenes. While the picture was filmed in black and white, the Wayne sequences were shot in color, "a device employed to develop the plot."

Running time: 84 minutes
Release date: May 23, 1958

219

The Barbarian and the Geisha

20th CENTURY FOX

CAST:

John Wayne, Eiko Ando, Sam Jaffe, So Yamamura, Norman Thomson, James Robbins, Morita, Kodaya Ichikawa, Hiroshi Yamato, Tokujiro Iketaniuchi, Fuji Kasai, Takeshi Kumagai.

CREDITS:

Produced by Eugene Frenke. Directed by John Huston. Screenplay by Charles Grayson. Story by Ellis St. Joseph. Photographed by Charles G. Clarke, ASC. Edited by Stuart Gilmore, ACE. Art direction by Lyle R. Wheeler and Jack Martin Smith. Assistant direc-tor: Joseph E. Rickards. Music by Hugo Friedhofer. Sound by W. D. Flick and Warren B. Delaplain. Script supervisor: Teinosuke Kinugasa. Assistant to the producer: Paul Nakaoka. Color by DeLuxe. Filmed in CinemaScope.

SYNOPSIS:

For two hundred years Japan has been "the forbidden empire," turning away all foreigners and abusing and killing shipwrecked mariners.

But now, 1856, a U.S. Navy frigate appears on the horizon, and as the excited Shimoda populace lines the waterfront, a longboat slowly makes its way toward shore, carrying Townsend Harris (John Wayne), first accredited U.S. diplomatic representative to Japan. He is accompanied only by his interpreter, Henry Heusken (Sam Jaffe), and three Chinese servants. He is immediately ordered off Japanese soil, but defies the order and takes up residence in a ruined temple, infested with rats. The Japanese refuse to sell him any food and keep him under constant observation.

It is in this climate that Harris, to fulfill his commission by President Pierce, must make his way to the nation's capital, Yedo (Tokyo), and there negotiate a commercial treaty. Patiently, but stubbornly, Harris forces Tamura (So Yamamura), governor of Shimoda, to concede minor points. In an effort to spy on Harris, and perhaps distract him from his persistent pursuit of his mission, Tamura introduces into Harris' household as a servant, the lovely geisha, Okichi (Eiko Ando). She expects to be brutalized by Harris, but instead finds him to be a kindly, considerate man. Her own people, however, misunderstand her role and reject her.

To Harris' joy, at long last an American ship appears in the harbor, but Harris discovers cholera aboard and turns it away. Several sailors attempt to escape, however, and though rounded up promptly, they introduce the dread disease into Shimoda. Harris,

221

feeling responsible for this catastrophe, makes a valiant fight against the epidemic with the aid of Heusken and Okichi. The Japanese do not understand sanitation and Harris, after burning down some infected houses, is placed under close arrest. However, he succeeds in breaking the epidemic.

Tamura recognizes this accomplishment and feels bound, under the Japanese code of honor, to permit Harris to go to Yedo. In the capital, Harris finds the government widely divided on the question of the treaty. But patiently he brings the majority around to his way of thinking. The reactionary forces, seeking to preserve Japan's isolation, plot to kill Harris and designate the unwilling Tamura as their agent. Tamura, in turn, commands the assistance of Okichi who by now has come to love Harris.

Bound by tradition to obey, she springs the trap with herself, rather than Harris, as victim. But an accident reveals her identity and Tamura, his own internal turmoil becoming unendurable, commits suicide. Okichi, however, cannot buy happiness through breaking the Japanese code and flees from Harris. She watches sadly from the midst of the great throng as Harris rides into the imperial palace to complete his treaty.

Running time: 104 minutes
Release date: September 30, 1958

Ricky Nelson, John Wayne, and Dean Martin

Rio Bravo

An Armada Production

WARNER BROTHERS

CAST:

John Wayne, Dean Martin, Ricky Nelson, Angie Dickinson, Walter Brennan, Ward Bond, John Russell, Pedro Gonzalez-Gonzalez, Estelita Rodriquez, Claude Akins, Malcolm Atterbury, Harry Carey, Jr., Bob Steele, Myron Healey, Fred Graham.

CREDITS:

Produced and directed by Howard Hawks. Screenplay by Jules Furthman and Leigh Brackett. Photographed by Russell Harlan, ASC. Edited by Folmar Blangsted, ACE. Art direction by Leo K. Kuter. Music composed and conducted by Dimitri Tiomkin. Assistant director: Paul Helmick. Sound by Robert B. Lee. Color by Technicolor.

SYNOPSIS:

Sheriff John T. Chance (John Wayne), of the little bordertown of Rio Bravo, arrests Joe Burdette (Claude Akins) for the brutal murder of an unarmed man. But Joe's older brother Nathan (John Russell), most powerful rancher on the border, has his riders bottle

up the town so Chance can't get his prisoner out to the U.S. marshal or get help in. Professional gunmen hired by Burdette slip silently into town, watch Chance's every move and wait their ruthless employer's order to strike. Assisting him against this deadly campaign, the sheriff has only his regular deputy, old crippled Stumpy (Walter Brennan), and newly sworn Dude (Dean Martin), former deputy and famous gunslinger, now making a desperate effort to snap out of a two-year drunk in order to help his friend. Forced by Burdette's blockage to halt in Rio Bravo are Feathers (Angie Dickinson), alluring young stagecoach passenger, and a wagon train of fuel and dynamite operated by Chance's friend, Pat Wheeler (Ward Bond), and guarded by Colorado (Ricky Nelson), a quiet, young gunfighter.

The first victim of Burdette's gunmen is Pat Wheeler, shot in the back. Chance and Dude trail the murderer to a saloon, where they disarm eight Burdette men, and Dude shoots the killer as he is about to fire on them. Later, Dude is captured and Nathan Burdette makes his proposition: he will trade Dude for Joe. Chance sends word that he accepts, but at the exchange of prisoners, Dude downs Joe with a flying tackle and the fight is on. Stumpy comes to the rescue by setting fire to one of Wheeler's wagons of dynamite. The terrific blast quickly ends the battle, and Chance returns to Feathers for good.

Running time: 141 minutes
Release date: February 17, 1959

John Wayne and players

The Horse Soldiers

A Mahin-Rackin Production

UNITED ARTISTS

CAST:

John Wayne, William Holden, Constance Towers, Althea Gibson, Hoot Gibson, Anna Lee, Russell Simpson, Stan Jones, Carleton Young, Basil Ruysdael, Strother Martin, William Henry, William Leslie.

CREDITS:

Produced by John Lee Mahin and Martin Rackin. Directed by John Ford. Screenplay by John Lee Mahin and Martin Rackin. From the novel by Harold Sinclair. Photographed by William Clothier. Edited by Jack Murray. Art direction by Frank Hotaling. Music by David Buttolph. Color by DeLuxe.

SYNOPSIS:

The year is 1863, the month April. The Civil War has been going badly for the Union—they key stumbling block is Vicksburg, high on a bluff over the Mississippi River. Ulysses S. Grant has been sitting in front of Vicksburg for a year. If he doesn't take it before summer, he'll probably be there another year. If he can take it, then General Sherman can be turned loose, march to the sea, cut the Confederacy in two— and sooner than later, the bloodshed would be over and the war won by the Union.

Grant calls in Colonel Marlowe (John Wayne), dispatches him 300 miles into enemy territory to cut the railway line at Newton Station by destroying that railhead. This would dry up Vicksburg's supply line.

Colonel Marlowe takes off on his "horse ride" with an understrength brigade of Union cavalry. His men think they are on the way north for a parade. They learn different at daybreak, when they find the sun rising over their left shoulders.

The start is marred by friction between Marlowe and his surgeon, Major Kendall (William Holden). Marlowe has the expected contempt of the combat soldier for his colleague who carries no arms. In addition, when Kendall asserts his rights as an officer in the medical corps to declare unfit any soldier he considers so, Marlowe and Kendall clash. It doesn't help the situation any when Marlowe is reminded that regulations back up Kendall.

En route to Newton Station, Marlowe stops at a plantation where Hannah (Constance Towers), its beautiful owner, learns their plans. He is forced then to take her along with them for security reasons, beginning a hectic romance between violently opposing strong personalities.

Marlowe destroys Newton Station. Unable to return to La Grange, Tennessee, his starting point, he continues another three hundred miles through the heart of Rebel territory into Baton Rouge, then in Yankee hands, but fighting and running every inch of the way.

The climax comes at a bridge spanning the Amite River. To escape closely pursuing Confederate cavalry, Marlowe orders the bridge mined. Seconds before the bridge is destroyed, Marlowe gets across, leaving Hannah behind after fond vows to meet when the war is over.

Running time: 119 minutes
Release date: June 12, 1959

John Wayne, John Ford,
and Constance Towers

John Wayne, Richard Widmark, Laurence Harvey, and players

The Alamo

A Batjac Production

UNITED ARTISTS

CAST:

John Wayne, Richard Widmark, Laurence Harvey, Richard Boone, Frankie Avalon, Patrick Wayne, Linda Cristal, Joan O'Brien, Chill Wills, Joseph Calleia, Ken Curtis, Carlos Arruza, Jester Hairston, Veda Ann Borg, John Dierkes, Denver Pyle, Aissa Wayne, Hank Worden, Bill Henry, Bill Daniel, Wesley Lau, Chuck Roberson, Guinn Williams, Olive Carey, Rubin Pa-dilla, Carol Berlin, Tom Hennesy, Cy Malis, Rojelio Estrada.

CREDITS:

Produced and directed by John Wayne. Original screenplay by James Edward Grant. Music composed and conducted by Dimitri Tiomkin. Lyrics by Paul

Francis Webster. Photographed by William H. Clothier. Edited by Stuart Gilmore, ACE. Art direction by Alfred Ybarra. Sound by Jack Solomon. Special effects by Lee Zavitz. Technical supervision by Frank Beetson and Jack Pennick. Assistant directors: Robert E. Relyea and Robert Saunders. Color by Technicolor. Filmed in Todd-AO.

SYNOPSIS:

In 1836 Texas, then the northernmost province of Mexico, rebels against the tyrannical rule of General Santa Anna (Rubin Padilla) and declares itself a Republic. General Sam Houston (Richard Boone) is trying to raise and train an army before Santa Anna's advancing forces reach the Texas provisional government at Washington-On-The-Brazos. Colonel Travis (Laurence Harvey) arrives with 25 men to establish the first line of defense against Santa Anna. Colonel Jim Bowie (Richard Widmark) has also come to fight for Texas independence, with a small force of volunteers. A strong rivalry immediately develops between these two strong-willed men which threatens to develop into a private war, but much of their differences are mediated by Colonel Davy Crockett (John Wayne). Including a group of Mexican volunteers, these one hundred eighty men prepare to stand against the advancing Mexican army in a one-time Spanish mission now crumbling into ruin. It is the only fortress

John Wayne and Linda Cristal

from which to hold off the 7000 troops marching against Houston, and give the general time to raise his army.

In San Antonio, Crockett meets and romances Flaca (Linda Cristal), a beautiful Mexican widow. Truly in love with her, he nevertheless sends her away before the fighting begins. When Santa Anna arrives in force and demands surrender, Travis answers with a cannon shot, and the legendary battle of The Alamo starts.

During a night patrol to destroy the Mexican's heavy cannon, Bowie is thrown from his horse and is saved by his young friend Smitty (Frankie Avalon). Altogether, the siege of The Alamo takes 13 days, during which the hope of the defenders is lost. James Bonham (Patrick Wayne) returns from his mission to get aid with the news that reinforcements have been ambushed and will not come. The Alamo is doomed. Travis offers the men a chance to retreat with honor, but explains to them how important their defense of The Alamo is. To a man, they all volunteer to remain,

and to a man they are all killed in the final bloody charge. Travis is shot, defending his position; Crockett is run through by a lance and manages to destroy the remaining powder and ammunition by blowing it up and himself along with it. Bowie, crippled by a previous wound, is propped up in a corner of the infirmary, and fires two guns before he is pierced by a dozen bayonets. Only Mrs. Dickinson (Joan O'Brien), her daughter and a Negro slave boy survive to provide the eyewitness story of the day-to-day events of the siege of The Alamo.

Forty-six days later, shouting the battle-cry of "Remember the Alamo," General Houston's army of 783 hurriedly-trained Texans surprised Santa Anna's forces at San Jacinto, and completely annihilated the Mexican general's dream of empire. It was only a short time later that the people of Texas rallied under Houston's leadership and formed the State of Texas.

Running time: 199 minutes
Release date: October 24, 1960

John Wayne and Linda Cristal

North to Alaska

20th CENTURY-FOX

CAST:

John Wayne, Stewart Granger, Ernie Kovacs, Fabian, Capucine, Mickey Shaughnessy, Karl Swenson, Joseph Sawyer, Kathleen Freeman, John Qualen, Stanley Adams, Stephen Courtleigh, Douglas Dick, Jerry O'Sullivan, Ollie O'Toole, Frank Faylen, Esther Dale, Richard Deacon, Kermit Maynard, Lilyan Chauvin, Joey Faye, Arlene Harris, James Griffith.

CREDITS:

Produced and directed by Henry Hathaway. Screenplay by John Lee Mahin, Martin Rackin and Claude Binyon. Based on the play *Birthday Gift* by Laszlo Fodor, from an idea by John Kafka. Photographed by Leon Shamroy, ASC. Edited by Dorothy Spencer. Special photographic effects by L. B. Abbott, ASC.

Art direction by Duncan Cramer and Jack Martin Smith. Music by Lionel Newman. Assistant director: Stanley Hough. Color by DeLuxe. Filmed in Cinema-Scope.

SYNOPSIS:

Sam McCord (John Wayne) and his partner George Pratt (Stewart Granger) have struck it rich in the gold rush in Alaska. Sam plans to use the money to travel to Seattle to buy mining machinery for enhancing his chances at more gold, and bring back his partner's fiancee, while George stays in Alaska to build a honeymoon cabin for the bride.

Before Sam can get away he meets a fast-talking confidence man, Frankie Canon (Ernie Kovacs), who offers him a counterfeit diamond ring as security on a $500 loan. The fight that ensues is topped by more trouble for Sam when George's younger brother Billy (Fabian) tries to sail on the barge with him. Sam throws the boy overboard and leaves for Seattle alone, unaware that in his absence the cunning Frankie Canon has befriended George and the boy, selling them another diamond ring for George's fiancée Jennie.

Meanwhile, in Seattle, Sam finds to his surprise that his friend's beloved is already married to a coachman. Saddened by what he must tell George, he takes refuge in a honky tonk, where he meets the alluring Michelle (Capucine), a young lady eager to make as much profit from his generosity as possible.

When the time comes to return to Alaska, Sam becomes depressed again at the thought of breaking the bad news to George. He has a sudden idea: He will take Michelle back to Alaska as a replacement for Jennie. Michelle agrees to go, thinking Sam really means her for himself.

Aboard ship next morning Michelle learns the truth and, heartbroken, throws the money Sam offers

as compensation through a porthole. By the time they reach the dock in Nome, they learn of trouble at the mine and Michelle is taken to a hotel now owned by Frankie, who, it is surprisingly revealed, is her former lover. Frankie wants to continue the relationship and use Michelle as a trap to steal Sam's mine, but she rejects the idea. Frankie, however, hears the alcoholic hotel porter Boggs (Mickey Shaughnessy) brag about once running a trapline across Sam's property and sees his chance to jump the partners' claim.

At the mine, Sam and Michelle find George gone to defend an adjoining mine against claim jumpers. Sam leaves to help, and Michelle is left alone with Billy, who is just discovering women. George and Sam run the outlaws away and return to deal with Billy. George is so upset at Sam's news of Jennie he calls Michelle a tramp and throws them both out. Michelle tells George the whole story of how Sam brought her as a kind gesture and how she tricked him into taking her to the mines. George, in a forgiving mood, con-

John Wayne, Fabian, and Capucine

ceives a way for her to be with Sam, but their plans backfire and turn both Sam and Billy against them.

Before Sam can leave, a troop of soldiers rides up announcing the gold mine has been impounded because of a cross-filing on the claim. Sam refuses to listen to George and Michelle and winds up in handcuffs when he tries to take his share of the gold. Michelle, fed up with the whole thing, returns to Nome to await departure for Seattle.

Meanwhile, Sam discovers that Boggs is behind the cross-filing and in the scenes that follow, the three partners are re-united in an effort to right the wrong. On their way to take Boggs to the authorities, they encounter Frankie and a fight ensues through the streets of Nome.

As the partners smash the culprits to the ground, the whistle blows, announcing Michelle's departure. Sam, accompanied by his partners, confesses his love at the last minute and Michelle stays with her new friends.

Running time: 122 minutes
Release date: November 7, 1960

John Wayne, Ina Balin, and Stuart Whitman

The Comancheros

20th CENTURY-FOX

CAST:

John Wayne, Stuart Whitman, Ina Balin, Nehemiah Persoff, Lee Marvin, Michael Ansara, Pat Wayne, Bruce Cabot, Joan O'Brien, Jack Elam, Edgar Buchanan, Henry Daniell, Richard Devon, Steve Baylor, John Dierkes, Roger Mobley, Bob Steele, Luisa Triana, Iphigenie Castiglioni, Aissa Wayne, George Lewis.

CREDITS:

Produced by George Sherman. Directed by Michael Curtiz. Screenplay by James Edward Grant and Clair Huffaker. Based on the novel by Paul I. Wellman. Photographed by William H. Clothier. Edited by Louis Loeffler. Action sequences directed by Cliff Lyons. Art direction by Jack Martin Smith and Alfred Ybarra. Music by Elmer Bernstein. Orchestration by Leo Shuken and Jack Hayes. Assistant director: Jack R. Berne. Sound by Alfred Bruzlin. Color by DeLuxe. Filmed in CinemaScope.

SYNOPSIS:

Gambler Paul Regret (Stuart Whitman) kills a man in an illegal gun duel in New Orleans in 1843. Avoiding arrest, he heads for Texas via riverboat. Aboard he has an affair with a beautiful adventuress, Pilar (Ina Balin).

Arriving at Galveston, Regret is greeted by Texas Ranger Captain Jack Cutter (John Wayne). Cutter takes Regret into custody and the two start a long

saddle trek to the Louisiana border Ranger Station. Regret makes one ineffectual attempt to escape, but on a second occasion he catches Cutter off guard and wallops him with a shovel.

Cutter returns to Ranger headquarters without Regret. He is informed that The Comancheros, a ruthless outlaw band supplying liquor and guns to the Comanches, have incited the Indians to attack. As luck would have it, a gun smuggler who dealt with the band has been arrested and Cutter volunteers to assume his identity in order to penetrate the outlaw stronghold.

Cutter, driving a wagonload of guns, stops at a small town near the Comancheros' hideout. He is approached by gun-runner Tully Crow (Lee Marvin) and accepts Crow's offer of partnership on a gun deal. Cutter is surprised to find Regret among a group of card players which he and Crow join and is amazed that Regret does not reveal the Ranger's true identity. Crow, drunk and losing heavily, wildly draws his guns, forcing Cutter to shoot him down in self-defense.

John Wayne and Stuart Whitman

Regret agrees to being placed under arrest and Cutter takes him to the near-by Schofield ranch, where a small group of Rangers is waiting. One Ranger, Tobe (Pat Wayne), informs Cutter that the Comanches will attack any moment. The Indians make their assault, but are repelled by the Rangers. A strong assist is given by Regret, an action that vindicates his past deeds and prompts his appointment as a Texas Ranger.

Regret and Cutter set out for the Comanchero stronghold, passing through a pillaged town on their way. Using the ruse of being rum-runners, they gain entrance into the hide-out. To Regret's surprise and regret, the daughter of the Comanchero chieftain (Nehemiah Persoff) is Pilar, the object of his riverboat romance. Regret expresses his love for her and she decides to join him and Cutter in their fight against her evil father. Pilar accompanies the two Rangers as they battle their way out of the stronghold. Cutter sets the Comanchero gun powder magazine afire as a delaying action. The whole village is in flames as they race for safety.

Believing they are out of danger, Cutter, Regret and Pilar quickly take cover when the cries of blood-thirsty Comanches are heard.

The Rangers have been following the tracks of the Indians. They see the smoke of the burning Comanchero settlement. A battle ensues. As Cutter joins the Rangers in defeating the Comanches and the renegades, he sees Regret and Pilar escape—and wishes them luck.

Running time: 107 minutes
Release date: October 30, 1961

Lee Van Cleef, Lee Marvin, James Stewart, and John Wayne

The Man Who Shot Liberty Valance

A John Ford Production

PARAMOUNT PICTURES

CAST:

John Wayne, James Stewart, Vera Miles, Lee Marvin,
Edmond O'Brien, Andy Devine, Woody Strode, John
Qualen, Jeanette Nolan, Lee Van Cleef, Strother
Martin, Ken Murray.

CREDITS:

Produced by Willis Goldbeck. Directed by John Ford.
Screenplay by James Warner Bellah and Willis Goldbeck. Photographed by William Clothier. Unit production manager: Don Robb. Edited by Otho Lovering. Art direction by Eddie Imazu. Assistant director:
Wingate Smith. Sound by Philip Mitchell.

SYNOPSIS:

Senator Ranse Stoddard (James Stewart) and his
wife, Hallie (Vera Miles), return to the small Western
town of Shinbone for the funeral of an old friend—
one Tom Doniphon (John Wayne). They arrive un-
announced except to a few of their old friends still
alive, including Link Appleyard (Andy Devine) and

Pompey (Woody Strode). An excited reporter presses the senator to explain why he traveled all the way from Washington to attend the funeral of a nobody. After a questioning look at Hallie, Ranse takes the man aside and tells the complete story, flashing back to the time he, Tom, the others—and Shinbone—were young.

Arriving in Shinbone when it was a territorial town, Ranse is robbed and beaten by Liberty Valance (Lee Marvin), brutal gunman employed by a clique of powerful cattlemen who oppose statehood for the Territory. Ranse is found by Tom Doniphon, a quiet, respected rancher and the only person with whom Valance is afraid to tangle. He and his faithful employee, Pompey, get Ranse to a cafe operated by a kindly Swedish couple, Peter (John Qualen) and Nora (Jeanette Nolan), who take care of the injured tenderfoot and give him a job in their kitchen. There he meets Hallie, a pretty waitress linked romantically with Tom.

Determined to bring law, order and statehood to the Territory, Ranse hangs out his lawyer's shingle at the office of Dutton Peabody (Edmond O'Brien), newspaper editor, despite Tom's warning that Liberty Valance will return to Shinbone and kill him. The pot begins to boil when Ranse and Peabody win out over Valance as delegates to the Territorial Convention to fight for statehood.

Enraged, Valance retaliates after the meeting by brutally beating Peabody and wrecking his office. Ranse gets a pistol, which he doesn't know how to use, and starts out after Valance. The terrified Hallie, now in love with the young lawyer, appeals to Tom to save him. Liberty and Ranse meet in the street at night; there is a burst of gun-fire and Valance falls dead.

During an emotional aftermath Tom learns of Hallie's feeling for Ranse. Bitterly disappointed, he burns down the addition to his ranch house he has been building for her.

Andy Devine, John Wayne, Jeanette Nolan, John Qualen, James Stewart, and Vera Miles

On the strength of being "the man who shot Liberty Valance," a reputation he detests, Ranse Stoddard is nominated at the Territorial Convention to run for congress against the cattlemen's candidate. When, unable to face a career built on a killing, he leaves the convention hall. Tom tells him the truth: that it was he who shot Liberty Valance, in the darkness of the street, and he did it only for Hallie. And for Hallie, Ranse must continue to take the credit for the killing and accept the nomination. This Ranse does.

He wins the election, goes to Washington to lead the successful fight for statehood and is nominated for governor. Again he is going to refuse and again Tom suddenly appears and urges him to accept, for Hallie's sake. And thus Tom becomes Ranse's conscience, the force which drives him to the U.S. Senate and a brilliant career in Washington.

At the conclusion of Ranse's story, the reporter slowly tears up his notes. Ranse asks, "You're not going to use the story?" The reporter answers, "No, sir. As our late and great editor, Dutton Peabody, used to say: 'It ain't news. This is the West. When the legend becomes a fact, print the legend!'"

Running time: 123 minutes
Release date: April 11, 1962

REVIEW:

"The B-Western costumes, the simplicity of movement and composition of William Clothier's black and white photography, the thoroughgoing brutality of Lee Marvin's villain, all combine to make *The Man Who Shot Liberty Valance* look like *The Western*. As for the principals, Stewart—skinny, stammering, sincere and befuddled—is *the* Jimmy Stewart; Wayne—taciturn, good-natured, tough and supremely confident—is *the* John Wayne."

Du Pré Jones, *Sight and Sound*

Woody Strode, John Wayne, Vera Miles, and James Stewart

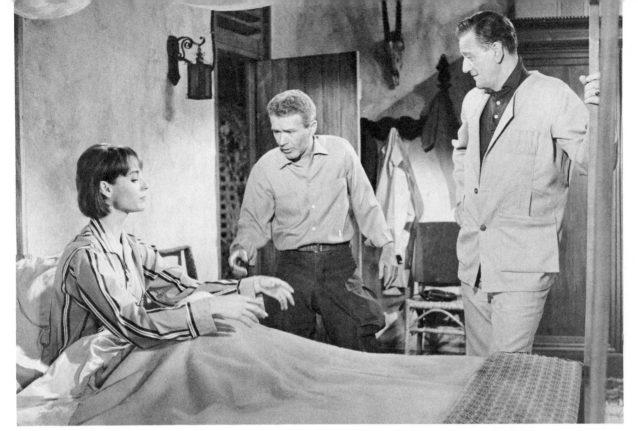

Elsa Martinelli, Red Buttons, and John Wayne

Hatari

A Malabar Production

PARAMOUNT PICTURES

CAST:

John Wayne, Hardy Kruger, Elsa Martinelli, Red Buttons, Gerard Blain, Michele Girardon, Bruce Cabot, Valentin De Vargas, Eduard Franz, Queenie Leonard.

CREDITS:

Produced and directed by Howard Hawks. Screenplay by Leigh Brackett. From a story by Harry Kurnitz. Music scored by Henry Mancini. Color by Technicolor. Photographed by Russell Harlan. Edited by Stuart Gilmore.

SYNOPSIS:

Momella Game Farms in Tanganyika has long been known to zoos all over the world as one of the most reliable game-catching farms in East Africa. But with the owner now dead, only his attractive daughter, Brandy (Michele Girardon) is left to carry on.

A group of restless catchers have stayed on to help her. Leader of this devil-may-care group is Sean Mercer (John Wayne), an American, veteran of a hundred game chases. There is also Kurt Stahl (Hardy Kruger), a former racing driver, and Pockets (Red Buttons), a former New York taxi driver.

Into this tightly knit group comes a photographer, not a man, as Sean had expected, but an attractive woman, Serafina d'Allesandro, nicknamed Dallas. Dallas (Elsa Martinelli) is to photograph all the exciting action of game catching, which infuriates Sean, who feels that a woman has no place in such a dangerous operation. Her arrival, too, is badly timed, as one of the group has been critically hurt. During a rhino chase Indian (Bruce Cabot) has been gored by the charging beast. And even as Indian lies in a hospital,

Elsa Martinelli and John Wayne

a self-assured Frenchman, Chip Maurey (Gerard Blain), arrives to ask for Indian's job.

Chip's request for the job infuriates Kurt and Luis (Valentin de Vargas), Argentine member of the group. In anger, Kurt knocks Chip down. Sean intervenes, explaining that they need an extra hand, and after Chip proves he can take care of himself, he is hired.

Complicating matters, as far as Sean is concerned, is Dallas' acquisition of a baby elephant, then a second, then a third. Sean points out the danger that the young elephants may attract the main herd, but Dallas wins her point.

In a furious chase after wildebeeste, Kurt's jeep overturns, injuring both Kurt and Chip. But when Brandy arrives at the scene of the accident, her concern, if any is well hidden. However, the next day, when Pockets accidentally falls from a fence, she betrays her real romantic feelings by rushing up to comfort him.

Red Buttons, John Wayne, and Valentine De Vargas

Once again out for rhino, Sean spots a big one, which Indian says resembles the one that gored him. After a long and dangerous chase, they rope the animal and are ready to crate it, when it escapes. The group narrowly avoid disaster, then pursue the rampaging beast, and finally recapture it, breaking what Indian calls his rhino jinx.

Back at the farm, Sean is furious when he discovers that Dallas has left. He loads one of the baby elephants into a jeep to act as bloodhound. He sets off after Dallas, the other two elephants following behind. The pursuit through the small town of Arusha rivals a tornado. The elephants relentlessly track down Dallas, chase her through streets, alleys, stores, and finally corner her inside the town hotel. Tearfully Dallas agrees to return with Sean.

That night Sean discovers Dallas in his bed. As he is about to join her, since they were married that afternoon, there is a trumpeting and stampeding. The three baby elephants crash into the room, also eager to join Dallas in bed!

Running time: 157 minutes
Release date: May 24, 1962

The Longest Day

20th CENTURY-FOX

CAST:

John Wayne, Robert Mitchum, Henry Fonda, Robert Ryan, Rod Steiger, Robert Wagner, Richard Beymer, Mel Ferrer, Jeffrey Hunter, Paul Anka, Sal Mineo, Roddy McDowall, Stuart Whitman, Steve Forrest, Eddie Albert, Edmond O'Brien, Fabian, Red Buttons, Tom Tryon, Alexander Knox, Richard Burton, Kenneth More, Peter Lawford, Richard Todd, Leo Genn, John Gregson, Sean Connery, Curt Jurgens, Werner Hinz, Paul Hartmann, Gert Froebe, Hans Christian Blech, Wolfgang Preiss, Peter Van Eyck, Arletty, Jean-Louis Barrault, Bourvil, Pauline Carton, Ray Danton,

Irina Demich, Henry Grace, Peter Helm, Donald Houston, Karl John, Fernand Ledoux, Christian Marquand, Dewey Martin, Michael Medwin, Richard Munch, Leslie Phillips, Ron Randell, Madeleine Renaud, Georges Riviere, Norman Rossington, Tommy Sands, George Segal, Jean Servais, Richard Wattis, Georges Wilson.

CREDITS:

Produced by Darryl F. Zanuck. Directed by Ken Annakin, Andrew Martin and Bernhard Wicki. Screenplay by Cornelius Ryan. Additional episodes by Romain Gary, James Jones, David Pursall and Jack Seddon. Based on the book by Cornelius Ryan. Photographed by Jean Bourgoin, Henri Persin and Walter Wottiz. Filmed in CinemaScope.

SYNOPSIS:

"The Longest Day" is June 6, 1944, the day Europe waited for since Hitler's armies overran the continent.

Combined American, British and Canadian forces assault the beaches of Normandy in an effort to gain a foothold on the continent. From the viewpoint of the Americans and Germans involved, the story unfolds through numerous episodes highlighting the Longest Day. John Wayne portrays Lt. Col. Benjamin Vandervoot, American officer.

Running time: 180 minutes
Release date: October 3, 1962

John Wayne and Henry (Harry) Morgan

How the West Was Won

METRO-GOLDWYN-MAYER and CINERAMA

CAST:

Carroll Baker, Lee J. Cobb, Henry Fonda, Carolyn Jones, Karl Malden, Gregory Peck, George Peppard, Robert Preston, Debbie Reynolds, James Stewart, Eli Wallach, John Wayne, Richard Widmark, Brigid Bazlen, Walter Brennan, David Brian, Andy Devine, Raymond Massey, Agnes Moorehead, Henry (Harry) Morgan, Thelma Ritter, Mickey Shaughnessy, Russ Tamblyn, Lee Van Cleef, Rodolfo Acosta, Jay C. Flippen, Joseph Sawyer. Narrator: Spencer Tracy.

CREDITS:

Produced by Bernard Smith. Directed by Henry Hathaway, John Ford and George Marshall. Written by James R. Webb. Suggested by the series "How the

244

West Was Won" in *Life* Magazine. Photographed by
William H. Daniels, ASC, Milton Krasner, ASC,
Charles Lang, ASC and Joseph LaShelle, ASC. Edited
by Harold F. Kress, ACE. Music by Alfred Newman.
Art direction by George W. Davis, William Ferrari
and Addison Hehr. Second unit photography by Har-
old E. Wellaman, ASC. Assistant directors: George
Marshal, Jr., William McGarry, Robert Saunders,
William Shanks and Wingate Smith. Special effects
by A. Arnold Gillespie and Robert R. Hoag, ASC.
Print by Technicolor. Filmed in Ultra Panavision.

SYNOPSIS:

Five interrelated episodes tell the story of a half-
century of America's Westward expansion, as seen
through the eyes of four generations of a pioneer
family. John Wayne appears as General Sherman in
the Civil War sequence.

Running time: 162 minutes
Release date: November 7, 1962

Lee Marvin, Mike Mazurki, Elizabeth Allen, and John Wayne

Donovan's Reef

A PARAMOUNT PICTURE

CAST:

John Wayne, Lee Marvin, Jack Warden, Elizabeth Allen, Cesar Romero, Dorothy Lamour.

CREDITS:

Produced and directed by John Ford. Cinematographer: William Clothier. Unit production manager: Don Robb. Art direction: Hal Pereira and Eddie Imazu. Film editor: Otho Lovering. Sound: Hugo Grenzbach.

SYNOPSIS:

This is the story of life on a South Pacific Island where two ex-Navy men, John Wayne and Jack Warden, have stayed following the Second World War. Wayne to operate a bar and night club known as Donovan's Reef, and Warden to marry a lovely Polynesian princess, raise a family, and carry on his medical practice. Another shipmate, Lee Marvin, arrives later, and he and Wayne continue their brawling friendship. Trouble comes with the arrival of beautiful, haughty Elizabeth Allen, to find her father, Jack

Warden, who had neglected to return home to Boston after the war. Warden's friends, including sultry Dorothy Lamour, an entertainer at Donovan's Reef, plot to save his reputation, and the results are dynamic, often hilarious, and always heart-warming.

Running time: 112 minutes
Release date: July 1963

John Wayne and Lee Marvin

John Wayne, Elizabeth Allen, and Lee Marvin

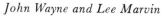

John Wayne and Lee Marvin

Stefanie Powers, Pat Wayne, John Wayne, and Maureen O'Hara

McLintock!

A Batjac Production

UNITED ARTISTS

CAST:

John Wayne, Maureen O'Hara, Patrick Wayne, Stefanie Powers, Yvonne De Carlo, Jack Kruschen, Chill Wills, Jerry Van Dyke, Edgar Buchanan, Bruce Cabot, Perry Lopez, Michael Pate, Strother Martin, Gordon Jones, Robert Lowery, H. W. Gin, Aissa Wayne.

CREDITS:

Produced by Michael Wayne. Directed by Andrew V. McLaglen. Original screenplay by James Edward Grant. Photographed by William H. Clothier. Edited by Otho Lovering. Sound by Jack Solomon. Music by Frank DeVol. Color by Technicolor.

SYNOPSIS:

George Washington McLintock (John Wayne), cattle baron, banker, and leading citizen of the territorial town of McLintock, has just about everything he wants except his wife, Katherine (Maureen O'Hara), who left him two years before because she suspected him of infidelities.

McLintock lives at his ranch house, attended by Drago (Chill Wills), general factotum of the place, and a Chinese cook, Ching (H. W. Gim). One of his closest friends is the storekeeper Birnbaum (Jack Kruschen), a confidant and chess opponent.

Among a group of impoverished homesteaders the other ranchers are trying to force out of the area,

McLintock finds a lovely, mature widow, Louise War-ren (Yvonne De Carlo), whom he hires as cook. She brings her seven-year-old daughter, Alice (Aissa Wayne); and he gives Louise's handsome son, Dev (Patrick Wayne), a job as cowhand. This tranquil state of affairs is suddenly disrupted by the return of Katherine McLintock, determined to make her husband consent to a divorce and to get custody of Becky (Stefanie Powers), their seventeen-year-old daughter, who is attending college in the East.

Becky returns from college and is immediately courted by Dev Warren and Matt Douglas, Jr. (Jerry Van Dyke), from Harvard. Their rivalry results in a fistfight. More trouble comes with the arrival of a band of bedraggled Indians to meet a train bearing their chiefs, just released from prison. When the chiefs refuse to be taken to Fort Sill, all the Indians are herded into a stockade by the ranchers, who don't want them around. McLintock does his best to prevent

John Wayne and Yvonne de Carlo

this, to no avail, especially after one of the chiefs is accused of kidnapping a white girl—a crime of which he is exonerated just in time to escape the gallows. With feeling running high, Bunny Dull (Edgar Buchanan), half-Indian town character, blows up the stockade and the Indians come pouring into town.

When this crisis calms down, Dev and Becky announce their engagement. And McLintock, roused to an exasperated fury by Katherine's stubbornness, chases his wife through the house, through the town and into a mud puddle where he takes her over his knee and gives her a solid spanking on her exposed pantaloons—after which he tells her to go get a divorce. Then, lo and behold, Katherine throws herself into his arms—and the McLintocks are together again.

Running time: 127 minutes
Release date: November 13, 1963

Maureen O'Hara and John Wayne

John Smith, Claudia Cardinale, Henri Dantes, John Wayne, and Lloyd Nolan

Circus World

A PARAMOUNT RELEASE

CAST:

John Wayne, Claudia Cardinale, Rita Hayworth, Lloyd Nolan, Richard Conte, John Smith, Henri Dantes, Wanda Rotha, Katharyna, Kay Walsh, Margaret MacGrath, Katherine Ellison, Miles Malleson, Katharine Kath, Moustache.

CREDITS:

Produced by Samuel Bronston. Directed by Henry Hathaway. Executive associate producer: Michael Wasznski. Music by Dimitri Tiomkin. Screenplay by Ben Hecht, Julian Halvey and James Edward Grant. Original story by Philip Yordan and Nicholas Ray. Photographed by Jack Hildyard and Claude Renoir. Assistant directors: Jose Lopez Rodero, Terry Yorke. Edited by Dorothy Spencer. Color to Technicolor. Filmed in Technirama.

SYNOPSIS:

It is the golden age of excitement, half a century ago, when American impresario, Matt Masters (John Wayne), decides to take his rambling Wild West show to Europe. His decision is swayed by the hauntnig desire to find Lili Alfredo (Rita Hayworth), who disappeared fourteen years earlier following the death of her husband, The Flying Alfredo. Lili had been in love with Matt, and it was believed at the time that Alfredo deliberately dove to his death when he realized his wife did not love him. Toni (Claudia Cardinale), the beautiful young performer raised by Matt, is actually Lili's daughter. She is infatuated with Steve McCabe (John Smith), one of the stars of Matt's Wild West show.

Giving their first performance on a ship while docked in Barcelona, a mishap hurls a trapeze performer into the water. The huge crowd surges to one side to see the performer in the water and causes the ship to keel over. In the chaotic pandemonium that follows, no lives are lost, but the disaster causes the untimely closing of the show.

Matt, now broke, leaves for Paris with Toni, Steve, and his longtime friend, Cap (Lloyd Nolan), to seek a job with Colonel Purdy's Wild West Show. After being hired, Matt secretly plans to put together his own show and signs up acts for his dreamed-up European tour slated for the following year.

First to be signed is a remarkable wire-walking act by Giovana (Katharyna), a 12-year-old girl, and her guardian, Tojo, the clown. Tojo is Aldo Alfredo (Richard Conte), formerly of the Flying Alfredos.

Now with his own show, Matt searches for Lili in Brussels, Vienna, Prague, Copenhagen, Rome, Milan,

and finally Madrid. At one of the final performances, Lili is in the audience. Tears blur her vision as she watches Steve and her lovely daughter, whom she has not seen since childhood. Cap notices Lili and tells Matt. At a reunion between Lili and Matt, after fourteen years, Lili insists on leaving until she is worthy of being Toni's mother.

At the winter quarters in Toledo, Spain, the romance between Toni and Steve blooms, but Matt accuses Steve of trying to use Toni as a leverage to become his partner.

Lili returns and gets a job with Matt's show without Toni knowing her identity. Neither Lili nor Matt realize that Tojo, the clown, who knows her real identity, is a menace.

In Vienna's Prater Gardens, Lili's identity and her husband's suicide is revealed to Toni by Tojo. Matt then forces Toni, heartbroken and hysterical, to listen to the truth—that Lili did not love her father and had begged him for a divorce.

Suddenly, there are screams, "Fire, Fire!" Matt and the performers fight to save the Big Top. Toni and Lili climb dangling ropes together and, after help-

ing to save part of the canvas, Toni turns to Lili embraces her. Steve comes up, puts his arms around both of them, and Matt's blackened face breaks into a smile.

The next night, Matt's show opens despite the fire. The packed house hears Matt Masters announce the new name of the Wild West show—The Masters and McCabe Combined International Circus—and call attention to "the two beautiful and brilliant ladies of the trapeze—Lila Masters and her daughter, Toni McCabe."

Running time: 131 minutes
Release date: June 26, 1964

John Wayne and Claudia Cardinale

The Greatest Story Ever Told

UNITED ARTISTS

CAST:

Max Von Sydow, Dorothy McGuire, Robert Loggia, Charlton Heston, Michael Anderson, Jr., Robert Blake, Burt Brinckerhoff, John Considine, Jamie Farr, David Hedison, Peter Mann, David McCallum, Roddy Mc-Dowall, Gary Raymond, Tom Reese, David Sheiner, Ina Balin, Janet Margolin, Michael Tolan, Sidney Poitier, Joanna Dunham, Carroll Baker, Pat Boone, Van Heflin, Sal Mineo, Shelley Winters, Ed Wynn, John Wayne, Telly Savalas, Angela Lansbury, Johnny Seven, Paul Stewart, Harold J. Stone, Martin Landau, Nehemiah Persoff, Victor Buono, Robert Busch, John Crawford, Russell Johnson, John Lupton, Abraham Sofaer, Chet Stratton, Ron Whelan, José Ferrer, Claude Rains, John Abbott, Rodolfo Acosta, Michael Ansara, Philip Coolidge, Dal Jenkins, Joe Perry, Marian Seldes, Donald Pleasence, Richard Conte, Frank De Kova, Joseph Sirola, Cyril Delevanti, Mark Lenard, Frank Silvera.

CREDITS:

Produced and directed by George Stevens. Produced in creative association with Carl Sandburg. Executive producer: Frank I. Davis. Associate producers: George Stevens, Jr., and Antonio Vellani. Screenplay by James Lee Barrett and George Stevens. Music composed and conducted by Alfred Newman. Sets created by David Hall. Art direction by Richard Day and William Creber. Screenplay based on the books of the Old and New Testaments, other ancient writings, the book *The Greatest Story Ever Told* by Fulton Oursler, and other writings by Henry Denker. Photographed by William C. Mellor and Loyal Griggs. Supervising film editor: Harold F. Kress. Edited by Argyle Nelson, Jr. and Frank O'Neill. Special effects by J. McMillan Johnson, Clarence Slifer, A. Arnold Gillespie and Robert R. Hoag. Second unit directors: Richard Talmadge and William Hale. Assistant directors: Ridgeway Callow and John Veitch. Sound by Charles Wallace. Choral supervision by Ken Darby. Color by Technicolor. Filmed in Ultra Panavision 70.

SYNOPSIS:

"The greatest story ever told" is the life of Jesus of Nazareth, from the cradle to the cross to resurrection. John Wayne portrays a centurion who leads Jesus to the crucifixion.

Running time: 195 minutes
Release date: February 15, 1965

255

Kirk Douglas, John Wayne, and Dana Andrews

In Harm's Way

An Otto Preminger Film

PARAMOUNT PICTURES

CAST:

John Wayne, Kirk Douglas, Patricia Neal, Tom Tryon, Paula Prentiss, Brandon De Wilde, Jill Haworth, Dana Andrews, Stanley Holloway, Burgess Meredith, Franchot Tone, Patrick O'Neal, Carroll O'Connor, Slim Pickens, James Mitchum, George Kennedy, Bruce Cabot, Barbara Bouchet, Tod Andrews, Larry Hagman, Stewart Moss, Richard Le Pore, Chet Strat-

ton, Soo Yong, Dort Clark, Phil Mattingly, Henry Fonda.

CREDITS:

Produced and directed by Otto Preminger. Screenplay by Wendell Mayes. Based on the novel by James Bassett. Photographed by Loyal Griggs, ASC. Special photography by Farciot Edouart, ASC. Second unit photography by Philip Lathrop, ASC. Edited by George Tomasini, ACE, and Hugh S. Fowler, ACE. Music by Jerry Goldsmith. Sound by Harold Lewis and Charles Grenzbach. Assistant directors: Daniel McCauley, Howard Joslin and Michael Daves. Filmed in Panavision.

SYNOPSIS:

The morning of Dec. 7, 1941, a quiet Sunday, is shattered by waves of Japanese planes bombing Pearl Harbor, sending warship after warship to the bottom of the ocean. Outside the Harbor, in open waters, a cruiser is having gunnery practice. It is this ship, commanded by Capt. Rockwell, called The Rock, Torrey (John Wayne) and his brooding executive officer Commander Paul Eddington (Kirk Douglas), that serves as temporary operational headquarters for the survivors of the holocaust. Among the few ships that escape is a destroyer helmed by Lt. (j.g.) Mac McConnel (Tom Tryon).

In the aftermath of the crucial blow, Torrey receives orders to gather his small armada and engage the enemy. Facing impossible odds and probable catastrophe, he violates orders and discontinues the required zig-zag patterns to conserve fuel. As a result, a lurking enemy submarine almost splits the cruiser in half with torpedo hits, and Torrey, who is injured, orders his forces to return to Pearl Harbor. For this

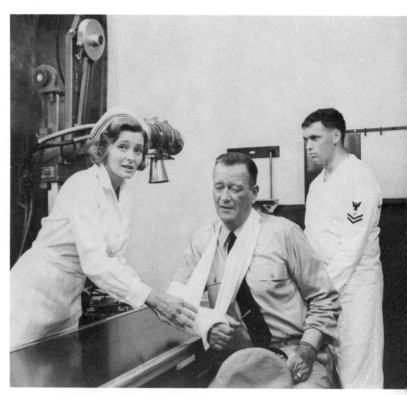

Patricia Neal and John Wayne

Kirk Douglas and John Wayne

Burgess Meredith and John Wayne

John Wayne and Paula Prentiss

action, he is severely reprimanded and reassigned to desk work.

Torrey watches forlornly as the American counter-offensive is formulated. During this time, he meets Maggie Haymes (Patricia Neal), a Navy nurse. It is she who informs him that his son, Jere (Brandon De Wilde), from whom he has been estranged for many years, is a naval officer on the island. The meeting between father and son is swift and bitter. Jere appears to be a young opportunist hoping to avoid his PT boat assignment by leading a soft staff job.

The initial shock of Pearl Harbor is absorbed and steady recovery is made. In a surprise, top-level meeting, Capt. Torrey is elevated to Rear Admiral. Now in a favorable light, Torrey is placed in command of Operation Skyhook, a spearhead mission designed to begin the drive against the enemy. Among those assigned to the operation are Eddington, McConnel, Maggie and Jere.

Torrey spends his few free moments with Maggie. Jere is less successful with his romantic attachment, ensign nurse Annalee Dorne (Jill Haworth). She is attracted to Eddington, who, on a picnic, vents his interior rage by brutally raping the young girl. Humiliated and shamed, Annalee commits suicide. Torrey breaks the news to Jere, and the tragedy serves to reunite father and son.

Jere returns to his PT boat command. Eddington, to redeem himself, defies orders, commandeers a reconnaissance plane and takes off alone to locate the lurking Japanese fleet in a certain death mission. Before he is shot down, Eddington radios the exact size and position of the enemy force which is heading on a course to intercept the U.S. invasion group.

The engagement between the two fleets is the first great sea battle of the Pacific war. Although the American task force fights superior odds and is largely destroyed, the Japanese retreat in confusion. Operation Skyhook is a success; a turning point in the war has been made. The victory, however, is costly, and among those who gave their lives was Jere.

Torrey, who was badly injured when his ship went down in a ball of flame, is sent home to recuperate. He will then return to the Pacific to command a new task force in the war against Japan.

Running time: 165 minutes
Release date: March 31, 1965

John Wayne, Dean Martin, Earl Holliman, and Michael Anderson

The Sons of Katie Elder

PARAMOUNT PICTURES

CAST:

John Wayne, Dean Martin, Martha Hyer, Michael Anderson, Jr., Earl Holliman, Jeremy Slate, James Gregory, Paul Fix, George Kennedy, Dennis Hopper, John Litel, Strother Martin, Rhys Williams, John Qualen, Percy Kelton, Rodolfo Acosta, James Westerfield.

CREDITS:

Produced by Hal Wallis. Directed by Henry Hathaway. Associate Producer: Paul Nathan. Screenplay by William H. Wright, Allan Weiss, and Harry Essex. Based on a story by Talbot Jennings. Photographed by Lucien Ballard, ASC. Edited by Warren Low,

ACE. Music by Elmer Bernstein. Art direction by Hal Pereira and Walter Tyler. Color by Technicolor. Filmed in Panavision.

SYNOPSIS:

Katie Elder bore four sons. The day she was buried they all return to the Texas town of Clearwater to pay their last respects. John (John Wayne) is the oldest, the toughest, the gunslinger. Texas, its bigness and its violence echoes in his empty soul. Tom (Dean Martin) is a different breed of hombre. He is good with a deck of cards and good with a gun—when he has to be. Matt (Earl Holliman) is the quiet one. Nobody ever called him yellow—twice. Bud (Michael Anderson, Jr.) is the youngest. Whatever hopes for respectability the Elder name has lies with him.

At the funeral are Sheriff Billy Wilson (Paul Fix) and his grim young deputy, Ben Latta (Jeremy Slate). They are both wary of the Elder brothers' arrival. Also at the burial, in addition to many townspeople, is the young woman Ben is courting, Mary Gordon (Martha Hyer), who keeps the rooming house.

In a little adobe house, John Elder and his brothers behold their mother's poverty. Mary visits, brings food, and is sardonic about the brothers' desertion of Katie. Only Bud, who has been going to college, shows a possibilty of becoming a fine, respected man.

As the brothers investigate into the past and present circumstances of their mother's life, they find the ranch is no longer hers and that she was penniless. John discovers that Pa Elder supposedly gambled away the ranch when he was drunk and that on the same night he was killed. The only witnesses are Morgan Hastings (James Gregory) and

his son, Dave (Dennis Hopper). The sheriff warns the Elders to stay out of trouble.

Realizing that the only tribute to Ma Elder would be for Bud to finish college, the brothers pledge themselves to that cause. Yet they feel the loss of the ranch was under peculiar circumstances, and decide to find out the truth.

The Hastings, in order to protect themselves and their illegal acquisition, and to cover the murder of Pa Elder, do everything possible to incriminate the brothers. Reputation being against them, the Elder boys quickly become suspect by the law. The sheriff is killed by the Hastings and the brothers are blamed. They give themselves up are taken, with a posse, to Laredo.

Unknowingly, Ben has sworn in deputies that are really Hastings men. They attempt to ambush the brothers and slaughter them. Matt Elder and Ben Latta are killed. The deputized guards who escaped tell they were ambushed by "John Elder's gang." The Elders return to town for a doctor for Bud, who has been wounded. The surging, angry crowd is

Earl Holliman, John Wayne, and Dean Martin

held back by John and Tom. Later, John tells the Judge what really happened and says they will surrender only to the U.S. marshal. The judge agrees to get the marshal from Laredo.

Under the cover of night, Tom sneaks away and captures Dave Hastings. The brothers try to get the truth. Morgan Hastings goes after the Elders to rescue his son, and shoots his own boy by mistake. Dying, Dave reveals that his father shot Ben, killed Billy and shot Pa Elder. The judge, in the next room, overhears. Dave dies and Tom, who has been mortally wounded, dies consigning Bud's future to John. John engages Morgan Hastings in a gun duel and kills him. Then he goes to the rooming house.

Mary is on the porch. She tells him Bud will be all right. As they pass inside, Mary's skirts brush Katie's rocker. It rocks contentedly.

Running time: 122 minutes
Release date: July 1, 1965

John Wayne, Dean Martin,
Martha Hyer, Michael Anderson,
and Earl Holliman

John Wayne and player

Cast a Giant Shadow

Mirisch-Llenroc Batjac

UNITED ARTISTS

CAST:

Kirk Douglas, Yul Brynner, Senta Berger, Angie Dickinson, Luther Alder, Stathis Giallelis, James Donald, Gordon Jackson, Haym Topol, Frank Sinatra, John Wayne, Ruth White, Michael Shilo, Shlomo Hermon.

CREDITS:

Produced, directed and written by Melville Shavelson. Co-produced by Michael Wayne. Based on a biography by Ted Berkman. Photographed by Aldo Tonti.

Edited by Gene Ruggiero. Art direction by Arrigo Equini. Sound by David Bowen. Special effects by Sass Bedig. Color by Technicolor. Filmed in Panavision.

SYNOPSIS:

Col. David Marcus (Kirk Douglas) is asked to train the rag-tag Israeli army into a first-class fighting machine to face the Arabs upon Israel's liberation.

Since he is an American citizen and still technically, an officer in the American army, Marcus is ordered—officially at least—by General Randolph

(John Wayne) not to accept. But the general knows too well that Marcus will do so anyway. So does his wife, Emma (Angie Dickinson).

In Isreal, Marcus meets the beautiful Magda (Senta Berger) and they are both magnetically attracted to each other. Marcus's wife won't divorce him, and Magda has declared her love and need for him.

Marcus is so successful in whipping the Israelis into a first-class fighting machine that he is made commander of all Isreali forces.

Later a troubled Marcus goes to tell Magda he realizes it is his wife he loves. Magda kisses him and then turns and walks out of his life.

At a Isreali outpost, Marcus is walking back from his meeting with Magda and one of his own sentries challenges him in the dark in Hebrew—a language Marcus has never mastered. He doesn't understand and continues walking. There is a shot and Mickey Marcus falls dead.

Running time: 142 minutes
Release date: March 30, 1966

John Wayne, Joanna Barnes, and Kirk Douglas

War Wagon

A Batjac Production—

A Marvin Schwartz Presentation

Released thru UNIVERSAL

CAST:

John Wayne, Kirk Douglas, Howard Keel, Robert Walker, Keenan Wynn, Bruce Cabot, Valora Nolan, Gene Evans, Joanna Barnes, Terry Wilson, Don Collier.

CREDITS:

Produced by Marvin Schwartz. Directed by Burt Kennedy. Screenplay by Clair Huffaker, based on his book. Assistant directors: Al Jennings and H. A. Silverman.

Music by Dimitri Tiomkin. Color by Technicolor. Filmed in Panavision.

SYNOPSIS:

Pierce (Bruce Cabot) defrauded Taw Jackson (John Wayne) of his gold-bearing land, shot and placed him in prison for some years. Now Taw has come out of jail on parole.

Taw plans vengeance on Pierce. He schemes to heist the armored-plated coach with Gatling guns mounted in a turret on top. Half a million in gold

264

John Wayne, Robert Walker, Howard Keel, Keenan Wynn, and Kirk Douglas

John Wayne, Kirk Douglas, and Howard Keel

dust is to be carried. For a $100,000 portion gunman Lomax (Kirk Douglas), who was hired to gun down Taw, is won over to Taw's side. Another ally is a canny Indian, Levi Walking Bear (Howard Keel). A third ally is a youthful drunk who's a wizard with dynamite, Billy Hyatt (Robert Walker). A fourth is the compulsive old thief Wes Catlin (Keenan Wynn) and his 18-year-old wife Kate (Valora Nolan).

Running time: 101 minutes
Release date: May 23, 1967

Kirk Douglas and John Wayne

Kirk Douglas and John Wayne

El Dorado

PARAMOUNT PICTURES

CAST:

John Wayne, Robert Mitchum, James Caan, Charlene Holt, Michele Carey, Arthur Hunnicutt, R. G. Armstrong, Edward Asner, Paul Fix, Johnny Crawford, Christopher George, Robert Rothwell, Adam Roarke, Chuck Courtney, Robert Donner.

CREDITS:

Produced and directed by Howard Hawks. Associate producer: Paul Helmick. Screenplay by Leigh Brackett. Based on the novel *The Stars in Their Courses* by Harry Brown. Photographed by Harold Rossen. Edited by John Woodcock. Art direction by Hal Pereira and Carl Anderson. Music by Nelson Riddle. Color by Technicolor.

SYNOPSIS:

In the Broken Heart Saloon at El Dorado, two old friends, each with a reputation, meet again. But J. P. Harrah (Robert Mitchum) greets Cole Thornton (John Wayne) with a pointed rifle. Harrah is sheriff now and according to his deputy, Bull Thomas (Arthur Hunnicutt), Thornton has been hired by rancher Bart Jason (Edward Asner) to take part in a range war.

Thornton admits Jason sent for him but he doesn't know why. Harrah explains that Jason is trying to

Robert Mitchum and John Wayne

take water away from Kevin MacDonald (R. G. Armstrong). Thornton says he will ride out to Jason's to turn the job down. As he leaves, he meets Maudie (Charlene Holt), who owns the saloon. She throws her arms around him, sees Harrah, and bursts out laughing when she finds her old flame and her current one are friends.

Warned that Thornton has gone to Jason's, MacDonald has posted his son Luke (Johnny Crawford) on a ridge with instructions to fire a warning if the gunman appears. Thornton is on his way back from Jason's when Luke wakes from a doze, sees him, and fires wildly. Thornton, thinking himself the target, shoots and drops the boy. Luke explains the error then, to escape the pain of his mortal wound, shoots and kills himself.

Thornton takes the body to MacDonald's place, finds the rancher with his other three sons, Saul, Matthew and Jared (Robert Rothwell, Adam Roarke, Chuck Courtney), and before he can explain what happened, MacDonald's daughter, Joey (Michele Carey), a wild thing in buckskin pants who has seen Luke dead, tries to shoot Thornton. She fails and rides off again in grief and fury.

As Thornton leaves, she ambushes him at a creek, dropping him with a rifle bullet. He manages to get back on his horse and escapes to Maudie's place,

John Wayne, Christopher George, and Edward Asner

John Wayne, Paul Fix, and Robert Mitchum

where Doc Miller (Paul Fix) treats him. The bullet is dangerously close to his spine, however, and Doc advises him to go to a better surgeon for removal. They move him to Harrah's house where Joey, having learned of Luke's suicide, calls to apologize. When he's well enough to travel, Thornton leaves El Dorado.

Months later, he is sitting in a cantina near the Mexican border. A young man (James Caan) nicknamed Mississippi, enters and calls one of the players at a card table by name, reminding him that he and three others had killed an old river gambler. He says he caught up with the other three and killed them. Now it was his turn to die.

Mississippi isn't wearing a gun, but kills the murderer with his knife. One of the other men, Milt (Robert Donner) goes for his gun, but Thornton steps in, draws faster and stops him.

The evident leader of the card-playing group is Dan McLeod (Christopher George), a fast gun. Thornton has heard of him. McLeod and his boys are going to El Dorado to work for rancher Jason and invite Thornton to join up, Thornton declines the offer.

When Thornton arrives in El Dorado, he finds Harrah stone drunk. Sickness overwhelms him and, temporarily, he can't perform his duties. Later, three McLeod men attack Jared MacDonald in Maudie's place. Jared is wounded. With shaking hands, Harrah buckles on his gun and returns to his duty. Thornton, Mississippi and Bull follow. There is a long gunfight and all three of McLeod's men are shot. Then Harrah arrests Jason, who appeals to McLeod for aid. Mc-

Leod refuses to help and is told to get out of town by Harrah, at noon the next day.

The McLeod gang ostentatiously ride out of town before the deadline. That night, McLeod and his men return and open fire on the sheriff's office, wounding Harrah in the leg. The next day, a sniper tries to kill off Mississippi and Bull. He misses and is chased by Thornton and Mississippi. Suddenly, the bullet near Thornton's spine pinches the nerve. He drops and, at that moment, Mississippi is hit over the head. McLeod and his men take their prisoners to the jail and offer to trade for Jason. Harrah accepts the trade.

Thornton's right hand is still partially crippled when, next day, Joey appears to report that Jason and McLeod are holding her brother Saul and will kill him unless her father signs over the water. Harrah hobbles aboard Maudie's buggy. Bull, seizing a bow and arrow, and Mississippi go with him. Thornton, realizing he can still work a rifle comes along.

Harrah stops the buggy. Mississippi jumps the man guarding the saloon's back door. Thornton rides up to the front in the wagon. McLeod is on the porch. Inside, Milt, who holding Jared, falls screaming with an arrow in his back. Harrah, Bull and Mississippi burst, firing, through the rear door. Thornton grabs his rifle and fires from under the wagon as McLeod draws and shoots. Thornton is hit in the leg, but he has killed McLeod. Their problems are ended.

Running time: 126 minutes
Release date: June 9, 1967

John Wayne and David Janssen

The Green Berets

A Batjac Production

WARNER BROTHERS—SEVEN ARTS

CAST:

John Wayne, David Janssen, Jim Hutton, Aldo Ray, Raymond St. Jacques, Bruce Cabot, Jack Soo, George Takei, Patrick Wayne, Irene Tsu, Edward Faulkner, Jason Evers, Mike Henry, Craig Jue, Luke Askew.

CREDITS:

Produced by Michael Wayne. Directed by John Wayne and Ray Kellogg. Screenplay by James Lee Barrett. From the novel *The Green Berets* by Robin Moore. Photographed by Winton C. Hoch, ASC. Edited by Otho Lovering. Music by Miklos Rosza. Sound by Stanley Jones. Second unit director: Cliff Lyons. Assistant director: Joe L. Cramer. Special effects by Sass Bedig. Color by Technicolor. Filmed in Panavision.

SYNOPSIS:

At the John F. Kennedy School for Special Warfare, Fort Bragg, North Carolina, the U.S. Special Forces—popularly known as the Green Berets—are being trained for guerrilla warfare in Vietnam. Colonel Michael Kirby (John Wayne), a dedicated career offices, selects two "A" detachments with Capt.

MacDaniel (Ed Faulkner). Among them are Master Sgt. Muldoon (Aldo Ray), Sgt. Doc McGee (Raymond St. Jacques), Sgt Provo (Luke Askew), and Louie Petersen (Jim Hutton), a persuasive promoter of supplies.

At headquarters near Anang, Kirby meets his Vietnamese counterpart, Colonel Cai (Jack Soo), who briefs him on a Strike Camp being built in Viet Cong territory. War Correspondent George Beckworth (David Janssen) joins "A" detachment as it leaves aboard four Caribou planes for the Strike Camp. Kirby suggests to Capt. Nim (George Takei), the Vietnamese camp commander, that a Seabee detachment will be needed to move the jungle further back to widen the "killing zone" around the camp. Mac-Daniel reports difficulty in recruiting Montagnard natives as strikers. so Kirby sends a helicourier to drop leaflets urging Montagnard natives to come down from the mountains to work and fight at the camp.

When the communications bunker and dispensary are hit a night mortar attack, Kirby reasons that the enemy have inside information. Next morning, Kirby and MacDaniel take off in helicopters to hunt the Viet Cong. They fly low over the jungle near the camp to draw VC fire, then they rout the enemy.

Later, during a vicious battle, correspondent Beckworth pitches in with the fighting men. Kirby lands his helicopters and runs with Muldoon through

John Wayne and players

heavy fire to the camp gate. Waves of VC are advancing, Kirby orders every mortar to defend the air strip to permit the landing of the Mike Force in their helicopters.

The Mike Force men fly in. What is left of the camp is retaken. Kirby prepares to rebuild. Help is already coming, as Montagnards wind down a trail to the camp.

Cai tells Kirby his plan to kidnap a communist leader. Phan Son Ti, using a seductive Vietnamese girl, Lin (Irene Tsu), as the lure and a small, hand-picked team for Ti's capture. Once at the plantation where Ti makes his headquarters, Kirby, Cai and several men overcome the guards capture the leader, and bring him and the girl to a rendezvous point. An Army Caribou plane brings them all back.

Running time: 141 minutes
Release date: June 17, 1968

John Wayne directing

John Wayne with camera crew

Hellfighters

UNIVERSAL PICTURES

CAST:

John Wayne, Katharine Ross, Vera Miles, Jim Hutton, Jay C. Flippen, Bruce Cabot, Edward Faulkner, Barbara Stuart, Edmund Hashim, Valentin De Vargas.

CREDITS:

Produced by Robert Arthur. Directed by Andrew V. McLaglen. Screenplay by Clair Huffaker. Photographed by William H. Clothier, ASC. Edited by Folmar Blangsted. Art direction by Alexander Golitzen and Frank Arrigo. Music by Leonard Roseman. Assisstant director: Terry Morse. Sound by Walson O. Watson, Lyle Cain and Ronald Pierce. Color by Technicolor. Filmed in Panavision.

SYNOPSIS:

Chance Buckman (John Wayne) is a rough-and-ready fighter of oil fires. His ex-wife, Madelyn (Vera Miles) has always loved him but could never stand the danger her husband faced in his profession. When the couples' only daughter, Tish (Katharine Ross) marries Chance's righthand man, Greg Parker (Jim Hutton), family fireworks erupt. Amid domestic dilemma, personal crisis, the intrigues of Latin-American politics, the thrill and risk of firefighting goes on.

Running time: 121 minutes
Release date: December 14, 1968

John Wayne and Vera Miles

John Wayne, Jim Hutton, and Edmund Hashim

Glen Campbell, John Wayne, and Kim Darby

True Grit

PARAMOUNT PICTURES

CAST:

John Wayne, Glen Campbell, Kim Darby, Jeremy Slate, Robert Duvall, Dennis Hopper, Alfred Ryder, Strother Martin, Jeff Corey, Ron Soble, John Fielder, James Westerfield, John Doucette, Donald Woods, Edith Atwater, Carlos Rivas, Isabel Boniface, H. W. Gim, John Pickard, Elizabeth Harrower, Ken Renard, Jay Ripley, Kenneth Becker.

CREDITS:

Produced by Hal B. Wallis. Directed by Henry Hathaway. Associate producer: Paul Nathan. Screenplay by Marguerite Roberts. From the novel by Charles Portis. Photographed by Lucien Ballard, ASC. Supervising editor: Warren Low, ACE. Production design by Walter Tyler. Assistant director: Willian W. Gray. Music by Elmer Bernstein. Title song lyric by Don Black. Color by Technicolor.

SYNOPSIS:

When Mattie Ross's (Kim Darby) father is murdered and robbed by his hired hand, Tom Chaney (Jeff Corey), Mattie aims to get vengeance without wasting too much time.

Mattie coolly out-deals Col. G. Stonehill (Strother Martin), horsetrader at Fort Smith, Arkansas, puts her father's finances in order and begins her search

276

for a man with "true grit." She finds and hires a hardbitten, whiskey-drinking, one-eyed U.S. marshal, Rooster Cogburn (John Wayne), to help her track down Chaney. Another younger and more handsome lawman, Texas Ranger La Boeuf (Glen Campbell), joins the search to collect the big reward money on Chaney's head for previous crimes commited in Texas. The two lawmen take an instant dislike to each other and the insults start flying left and right.

Rooster guesses that Chaney has joined Ned Pepper (Robert Duvall) and his outlaw band across the border. They pull a surprise raid on Pepper's hideout, kill four of his men and find their first clue—a gold piece stolen by Chaney from Mattie's father after the murder.

The search for Chaney and the remaining outlaws continues with half-drunken Rooster exchanging monumental insults with La Boeuf as they ride deeper into Indian territory. It's Mattie who finally stumbles into Chaney by accident. She manages to put a bullet

John Wayne and Kim Darby (in background)

into him before he takes her prisoner. Informed that the girl will be killed unless they leave the territory, Rooster and La Boeuf agree to retreat.

Just as Mattie is about to lose all hope, La Boeuf suddenly appears to rescue her while Rooster, gripping his horse's reins between his teeth, draws a pistol with one hand and holds a rifle in the other and charges directly into the entire band of outlaws. Meanwhile, just as Chaney smashes a rock into La Boeuf's head, mortally wounding him. Mattie gets another shot at Chaney, but the kick from her pistol sends her reeling backward into a pit where she breaks her arm and stirs up a colony of rattlesnakes.

Rooster kills Chaney and, with La Boeuf's dying help, gets Mattie out of the deep pit, but only after she'd been bitten by a rattler. Although wounded himself, Rooster wastes no time—not even to mourn the death of La Boeuf. In an incredible race against death, he runs horses into the ground with exhaustion, steals more without hesitation, carries Mattie in his

*Glen Campbell, John Wayne,
Dennis Hopper, and Jeremy Slate*

arms, until he is able to get her to a doctor in time to save her life.

When Mattie recovers, they meet again and, although she realizes that Rooster can never change his rascally ways, she knows that he still deserves to be a member of her family. But Rooster is still the wanderer, he mounts his horse, jumps a fence, just to show them he can still do it, and rides off into the winter sunset.

Running time: 128 minutes
Release date:

REVIEW:

"When the John Wayne retrospectives are in full swing, this will loom as one of his finest movie triumphs. Wayne steals the film in the role of the tough, colorful Rooster Cogburn."

William Wolf, *Cue*

John Wayne and Kim Darby

Antonio Aguilar, John Wayne, and Rock Hudson

The Undefeated

UNIVERSAL PICTURES

CAST:

John Wayne, Rock Hudson, Antonio Aguilar, Roman Gabriel, Marian McCargo, Lee Meriwether, Merlin Olsen, Melissa Newman, Bruce Cabot, Michael Vincent, Ben Johnson, James Dobson, Edward Faulkner, Harry Carey, Jr., Paul Fix, Royal Dano, Richard Mulligan, Carlos Rivas, John Agar, Guy Raymond, Don Collier, Big John Hamilton, Dub Taylor, Henry Beckman, Victor Junco, Robert Donner, Pedro Armendariz, Jr., Rudy Diaz, Richard Angarola, James McEachin, Gregg Palmer, Juan Garcia, Kiel Martin, Bob Gravage.

CREDITS:

Produced by Robert L. Jacks. Directed by Andrew V. McLaglen. Screenplay by James Lee Barrett. Based on a story by Stanley L. Hough. Music composed and conducted by Hugo Montenegro. Photographed by William Clothier, ASC. Edited by Robert Simpson, ACE. Art direction by Carl Anderson. Sound by Richard Overton and David Dockendorf. Unit production manager: Clarence Eurist. Assistant director: Jack Cunningham. Special photographic effects by L. B. Abbott, ASC. and Art Cruickshank. Filmed in Panavision. Color by De Luxe.

Rock Hudson and John Wayne

SYNOPSIS:

Col. John Henry Thomas (John Wayne) leads a Union cavalry charge on a Confederate position and overruns it after a sharp battle. At the moment of triumph a messenger arrives to report that Lee has surrendered and the Civil War has been over for three days. Thomas, together with his adopted son and bugler (Roman Gabriel), a Cheyenne Indian, and ten men who had come into the army with him, leaves the army and heads West where they propose to round up wild horses and sell them to the Federal forces.

In Louisiana, Confederate Colonel James Langdon (Rock Hudson), unwilling to accept life in a conquered land, leaves his plantation and departs for Mexico with his wife Margaret (Lee Meriwether), daughter Charlotte (Melissa Newman), Anne Langdon (Marian McCargo), the widow of his brother killed in the war, and a party of about a hundred men, women and children. Evading interception by Union troops, they cross the Rio Grande into Mexico.

Thomas rounds up his horses but finds the army contractors are swindlers and he sells them to agents of Emperor Maximillan, agreeing to deliver them near Durango, Mexico. The two parties cross trails and the Thomas group is able to save the Langdons from what most certainly would have been a massacre by the bandit Escalante (Pedro Armendariz, Jr.). This tends to ease the rather hostile reserve with which the Langdons have viewed the former Union soldiers, and Thomas and his group are invited to a Fourth of July party, which ends in a wild melee.

The Langdons arrive in Durango and are deceived and made captive by General Rojas (Antonio Aguilar), an ardent support of Benito Juarez and the foe of all who support Maximillan. Rojas says he will execute the Confederates unless Langdon persuades Thomas to turn over to him the horses so badly needed by the Juaristas. Thomas leaves the matter up to his men and, though it leaves them impoverished, they see no other way than to surrender the horses.

But there is another complication. Maximillan's agents summon a troop of French cavalry to take the herd by force. Using the 3,000 horses as a sort of battering ram, Thomas and Langdon overrun the French and deliver the herd to Durango. Rojas is true to his word and the Thomas and Langdon parties unite in the weary trek to an uncertain future at home.

Running time: 119 minutes
Release date: September 13, 1969

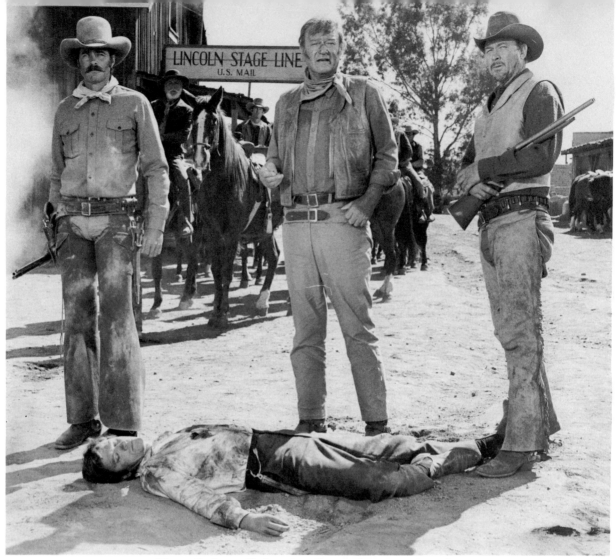

Glenn Corbett, Christopher George (on ground), John Wayne, and Ben Johnson

Chisum

WARNER BROTHERS

CAST:

John Wayne, Forrest Tucker, Christopher George, Ben Johnson, Glenn Corbett, Andrew Prine, Bruce Cabot, Geoffrey Deuel, Pamela McMyler, Patric Knowles, Richard Jaeckel, Lynda Day, John Agar, Lloyd Battista, Robert Donner, Ray Teal, Edward Faulkner, Ron Soble, John Mitchum, Glenn Langan, Alan Baxter, Alberto Morin, William Bryant, Pedro Armen-

dariz, Jr., Christopher Mitchum, Abraham Sofaer, Gregg Palmer.

CREDITS:

A Batjac (Andrew J. Fenady) production. Directed by Andrew V. McLaglen. Screenplay by Andrew J. Fenady. Photographed in Technicolor by William H.

Clothier. Edited by Robert Simpson. Music by Domi-
nic Frontiere. Art direction by Carl Anderson. Assistant director: Fred S. Simpson.

SYNOPSIS:

John Wayne is cast as John Simpson Chisum, an historical figure who was the largest owner of land and
cattle in the New Mexico territory around 1878. The
story is based on the bloody Lincoln County cattle war.
    Included in the story is the famous meeting of
Billy the Kid (Geoffrey Deuel) and Sheriff Pat Garrett (Glenn Corbett), culminating in the final con-
frontation between the two in which Garrett is gunned
down by the outlaw.

42

Forrest Tucker plays Lawrence Murphy, the ambitious, land-grabbing, power-hungry newcomer who was one of the principals in the infamous cattle war brought on by his challenging of Chisum's dominance and the latter's powerful resistance.

Patric Knowles plays the real-life character of an Englishman who befriends Billy the Kid and is murdered by Murphy's men. Bruce Cabot plays a sheriff under Murphy's domination, also an historical figure, Ben Johnson plays Chisum's grumbling foreman and friend, and Andrew Prine is a young banker and storekeeper.

Running time: 110 minutes
Release date: August 1970

Rio Lobo

NATIONAL GENERAL PICTURES

Released by Cinema Center Films

John Wayne and Jennifer O'Neill

As this book goes to press, John Wayne's 144th film, *Rio Lobo,* has not yet been released. Wayne plays an ex-Civil War officer who frees a Texas town of carpetbaggers and settles an old score with a wartime informer.

The film was directed by Howard Hawks, and the cast includes Jennifer O'Neill, Jack Elam, Jorge Rivero, Chris Mitchum, Dave Huddleston, and Peter Jason.

John Wayne, Jorge Rivero, and Jack Elam